100 Years Work

De'Amon Harges
Michael Mather
Seana Murphy

100 Years Work

Abingdon Press™
Nashville

100 YEARS WORK

Library of Congress Control Number has been requested.
ISBN: 9781791042455

Cover description: The cover shows a tree trunk with a network of roots splaying over the ground, all in shades of brown, yellow, and gold. The title, *100 Years Work,* and authors' names—De'Amon Harges, Michael Mather, and Seana Murphy—appear across the roots in dark yellow lettering.

MANUFACTURED IN THE UNITED STATES OF AMERICA

A Note from the Authors

II
The drowsy dawn from many a low-built shed,
Beheld his kindred driven to their task;
Late evening saw them turn with weary tread
And painful faces back; and dost thou ask
How sang these bondsmen? how their suff'rings mask?
Song is the soul of sympathy divine,
And hath an inner ray where hope may bask;
Song turns the poorest waters into wine,
Illumines exile hearts and makes their faces shine.
—Albery Whitman, from *Rape of Florida*, Canto I

In May 2020, the world witnessed the murder of George Floyd at the hands of a Minnesota police officer. Most astonishing was the fact that people literally watched as one man took the life of another. Heartbreak and outrage seized the global populace. Marches were organized; commercials proclaiming dedication to social and racial justice were made; aggressive diversity, equity, and inclusion policies were publicly adopted by large corporations; and study groups and book clubs sprang up all over the world. Yet no one questioned the historical significance of watching a Black man die at the hands of a white man; the historical and still active commission of lynching in the public square. Christians refused to draw the parallel between the death of this "other" at the hands of the state and the crucifixion of Jesus Christ. Astonishing.

Willful blindness is crippling communities. The willful decision by powerbrokers, social workers, religious leaders, and even family members to ignore the impacts of disparate distributions of wealth in this country on the lives of others led us to write this book.

Why now? Because our ancestors demand it. Why now? Because we carry the spiritual commandments of Christianity, African proverbs, aunts, and uncles who turned the "do unto others" motif into "do better with others—not for or unto others—and make the world a better place." Dr. Martin Luther King Jr. best answered the question in his "America's Promissory Note" speech (better known as the "I Have a Dream" speech): "We refuse to believe that the bank of justice is bankrupt. We refuse to believe that there are insufficient funds in the great vaults of opportunity of this nation. And so, we've come to cash this check, a check that will give us upon demand the riches of freedom and the security of justice."

This book speaks in three distinct voices because that's the only honest way to tell this story.

100 year work is not linear. Loving is not linear. We (the writers) are three distinct individuals with distinct experiences within triangulated time (past, present, and future). We could have blended our voices into one smooth narrative, but that would violate the very principles we're teaching. Real community work requires distinct voices in relationship, not homogenization.

We have written this book in three voices:

De'Amon Harges, the Social Banker—who learned asset-based community development from the inside, growing up in communities told they had nothing;

Michael Mather, the Experimenter/Social Inventor—a pastor who spent decades unlearning institutional assumptions and learning to see what is already present.

Seana Murphy, the Observer—trained to analyze institutions and power, who sees what deficit-based models miss.

Although this book has three voices, we are also one voice. A trinity, if you will. Each voice a chorus of our ancestors' hymns over melodies and rhythms, weaving together a delicious harmony. The voices share a singularity, a weaving of sorts: the belief in love. The belief in love is woven into each of our DNA. It is the positive manifestation of epigenetics.

Throughout this book, you'll hear each of us tell our stories and share our perspectives. Sometimes one voice will lead for pages. Other times we'll weave together. We've marked each voice clearly, with the person's name at the beginning of the section each of the authors writes. And when a new author begins you'll see that reflected in the name change. Find the harmony in the voices as you read.

Our hope is that in witnessing our stories, the abundance we see will cause your world to expand. Thank you for reading.

Who are we? Seana Murphy, The Observer
We are/I am Seana Murphy,
Daughter of Ernestine Wright
Daughter of Rosalie Hooper
Daughter of Callie Hooper
A Black woman who loves women, across all spectrums of love/loving—
mother of a beautiful Black son—
warrior and witness to the love existing in places that many are too afraid to acknowledge.

Trained in the philosophy of personalism, I believe that the personhood of God must be experienced first in the lives of people in community. This belief is guided by my full faith in the omnipresence of God and the ancestors.

Who are we? De'Amon, TORL, SB (The Original Roving Listener, Social Banker)
I am De'Amon Harges
We are sons of the South
Sons of Isham Dupree

Son of African ancestors, a slave in this country, owned by a ten-year-old

A father to our great-grandmother, Julia Taylor

Grandmother to our grandfather, Alec Braylock

We are descendants of Alec and Marie, whose union created my mother, Sharon Braylock.

We are here. I am here. Because of their journeys to escape the brutality and mistreatment of slavery, we journeyed to a not-so-promised land of South Bend, Indiana, onto sacred land, which became a toxic waste site.

This is responsible for me becoming a social banker, an imaginator, a weaver of community. This book is written by all of us. We are witnesses of healers and imaginators and social bankers. We want you to be writing your own stories along with us. We see you. This book is written because of our own new ways of seeing people working all day, acting on their own agency.

Who are we? Michael, the Experimenter/Social Inventor

I am Michael Mather

Son of Lillian Richter

Daughter of Lillian Brown

and George Richter

Son of Herbert Mather

Son of Essie Archerd

and Earl Mather

My father from Minnesota, my mother from Georgia, and though I was born in Brooklyn, I have been, like Seana and De'Amon, a longtime citizen of Indiana.

I'm a pastor, a father, a husband, a grandfather, a reader, a white guy. My friends know me as a storyteller; an observer; a witness. I have seen miraculous things in communities and places other people avoid or call "bad." They are the places where abundance, generosity, and love are most clearly seen. Why? Because when everything else is stripped away, what is left, is, the truth.

We are three people grateful for those we have been blessed to live and work among. So we say:

For my people standing, staring, trying to fashion a better way from confusion, from hypocrisy and misunderstanding, trying to fashion a world that will hold all the people, all the faces, all the Adams and Eves and their countless generations:

> Let a new earth rise. Let another world be born. Let a bloody peace be written in the sky. Let a second generation full of courage issue forth; let a people loving freedom come to growth. Let a beauty full of healing and a strength of final clenching be the pulsing in our spirits and our blood. Let the martial songs be written, let the dirges disappear.
> —Margaret Walker, "For My People"[1]

Contents

Introduction

Seana Murphy

Epigenetics of Joy

In 1942, Conrad Waddington coined the term "epigenetics." The term was used to describe the ways in which hereditary (gene expression) and environment work together. Since the coining of the term, social scientists have used the term to explain the impact of trauma on the development of humans in utero. The impact of continued systemic oppression, trauma in the Black community, and epigenetics have been explored and explained in a myriad of books, articles, and lectures. Tools have been developed to measure the negative impact of unjust environmental factors on the poor. It is important to note the specificity in the above statement. Wealthy people are not asked to complete such tools. Wealthy people do not encounter the assumption that their existence—down to their biological makeup—has been altered by traumatic experiences. Parenthetically, I find this curious: the concept of owning, controlling, and exploiting another human, a prerequisite of capitalism, must be borne out of a genetic expression that leads one to believe in one's own superiority over another. The ACES (Adverse Childhood Experiences Survey) is the most prominent tool used to quantify environmental trauma and the effects on human development.

While most studies continue to focus on the impact of trauma on gene expression, and because of this, the continuation of trauma responses across generations, very few focus on the epigenetics of joy. How does joy impact genetic expression? Why does trauma trump joy? In the last twenty-four years there have been 1,151 articles written on the topic of trauma and epigenetics. To date, there is no quantifiable number on the number of articles addressing the epigenetics of joy. Why is that? What would happen if the focus were on joy as opposed to trauma? Could the results of the focus on joy reveal what so many failed/fail to see? If we are to believe Newton's assertion that every action causes an opposite and equal reaction then it stands to reason that just as trauma negatively impacts genetic expression, joy positively impacts genetic expression.

The expression of joy in meals shared, songs sung, art created, and stories told are a few expressions of joy that transcend the physical environment. All these existed and continue to exist in "disadvantaged," "underserved," "underrepresented" (fill in the blank) communities. Why not focus on joy? Our hypothesis: focusing on joy dispels the idea of subjugation, humanizes the dehumanized, and gives credibility to the philosophy of personalism. God is omnipresent—even in spaces and places where God feels absent or invisible.

The genetic expression of joy, across 100 years, shapes how we see and move in the world. Remember this as we journey together.

In the 2020 documentary *The Hidden Life of Trees*, researchers documented the power of proximity related to healing. Trees have the ability to lend their energy to ailing trees, through their roots, as a way of saving the life of a tree. In order for the healing energy of one tree to save another, the roots must touch. 100 year work requires literal physical touch.

Many will remember learning how to calculate the age of a tree by counting the number of rings inside the stump. This elementary knowledge coupled with the new knowledge of how trees communicate and heal one another serves as a metaphor for this work. The manifestation of us, all of humanity, is a result of invisible energies that communicate and heal.

We humans represent rings of generations that have come before us. This fact, when centered into 100 years' work, gives rise to questions that we seek to answer through our unique voices and perspectives.

Immeasurable joy and love grounds this work. Belief in ancestral dreams, Langston Hughes's dream, grounds this work:

> I dream a world where all
> Will know sweet freedom's way
> —Langston Hughes, "I Dream a World"[1]

Parliament, the funk band's playful yet real urgency drives this work. Trust and believe, that 100 years work centers on one thing: "Turn this mother out!"

Preface

Seana Murphy

In this land—long before the ancestors spoke English—they read the stars; listened to the wind; followed moss on trees; listened to, smelled, and tasted the earth, searching. Without language, without knowledge of geography, without the basic human freedom of movement, they navigated God's creation—believing in a destination; believing in freedom.

Before the White Lion, there were villages filled with songs of celebration, traditions etched in memories, sorrows buried in the crevices of hearts, imperfect systems held together by beliefs in gods, ancestors, nature, and the universe. Before the White Lion, there was Black humanity.

After the White Lion, generations were forcibly bred-raped, murdered, and terrorized. The only histories taught were those of terrorized Black people or docile Black people. The white hero story of "letting former slaves" (fill in the blank) appeared in history books. The "some Black people owned slaves" narratives were used to justify slavocracy. In all of the twisted tales, however, the one tale that did not have to be told—because it was felt—is that in the midst of all of the unspeakable brutality, there was joy. Babies were birthed and named according to ancestral traditions. Little children, even after being sold away from their parents, made jokes, told stories, played games, and laughed. This fact is not a romanticization of resilience as this degree of resilience should not be required of any human! It is, however, a statement about spirit. Spiritual transcendence (cellular metamorphosis) all of this happened and continues to happen in the Black community; Black joy.

We are the culmination of many worlds. We are the culmination of complex humans that we call ancestors. We are the children of men and women who believed in a Christian God that favors the oppressed. We are the children of beautiful, calculating, smart, and courageous women. The women in our lineage were spiritual conquerors who embodied/embody the euphemism "make a way out of no way."

More than making a way out of no way, the women in our family's lineage found the calming balms in the music that still rings in our spirits. We love, celebrate, and aspire to be all that the women in our lives are (both on this planet and beyond).

The men in our lives were tenacious. The brutality of capitalism, racism, and wars (Vietnam and Korean) hardened them in such a way that to say that they knew how to love and give life completely would be to lie. Though love was present, it was expressed in ways that hurt. The absence of emotional connection hurt. The denial of physical affection hurt. These men, Black and white—one line born free—two lines born unfree, were connected by the psychology of dominance. Each in their own way tried but, unlike the women, they lacked the imagination needed to make a way out of no way.

Love has been the guiding force in our lives. It has been and will remain imperfect. A characteristic of the imperfection is the longing that we still have for the physical presence of those who now occupy the ancestral plane. We miss the laughter, the hard talks, the hugs, the hand holding, and most of all the constant assurance that everything will always be all right. We have lost grandparents, parents, aunts, uncles, and friends. We have curated romantic memories to keep their spirits alive in our hearts and spirits. We draw strength from these memories. It is through the memories we remind ourselves "weeping may endure for a night, but joy cometh in the morning" (Psalm 30:5 KJV). There are so many young people, mentors, church members, and others who have transitioned. We miss them. We love them. In the spirit of honoring them, we call their names:

Rosalie Hooper, Rev. Jicelyn Thomas, Dr. Rufus Burrows Jr., Sister Mari Evans, Jean Horth, Margaret Hadley, Abraham Brooks, Cousin Lisa, Carl "Buddy" Hurt, Grandma Dimple, Corey Roney, Mr. Goler, Carl Evans, Ms. Hintz, Parker Pengilly, Mr. Groves, Aunt Rosie. . . .

This is our love letter to the named and unnamed.

Through all of what will unfold in these pages, imagine what it took for Jesus to walk into the temple, face the money handlers and other power brokers, and to flip the tables over uttering words of total destruction! This is our faith. This is the faith that governs us and whatever your spiritual inclination, we hope that it is filled with divine urgency and power.

100 years of work is experienced. It is experienced in the mind, body, and spirit. The years are given life through stories. It is experienced as fixed. It is not. It is perspective. What happens across the time spectrum is shaped by the worlds that existed before us.

Perspective: Jesus lived, died, and was resurrected in less than forty years, but for Mary—his mother, immaculate conceiver of the embodiment of God—every day must have felt like 100 years lived.

Mary became pregnant as a teenager. Though nothing about her pregnancy is recorded, women who have given birth understand that it can feel like a lifetime before the baby is born.

Mary's child, Jesus, was born an outsider. Delivered in a manger, without doulas, doctors or nurses—just darkness, the stench of the animals, a man that she did not know or love, and random visitors that occupied the manger.

Mary gave birth to her son with a man that she did not choose as her husband. As a mother, like mothers today, Mary worried about her son. Mary loved her Son. The mother of the Son of God, Mary, like so many black mothers around the world, was helpless in the face of the violence that took her son's physical life from her. Valerie Castile, Tamika Palmer, Geneva Reed-Veal, Demetree Wynn, Sheneen McClain, are all Mary. Their names are not known to many however each of the women, like Mary, loved and lost their children to state sponsored violence. Their work is Mary's work: birthing, laughing, loving, praying, crying, and still believing in possibilities is 100 year work.

Perspective: According to white history, the Civil War lasted 4 years yet the wars for and against black humanity rages on in the minds, bodies, and spirits of those of us who are here and the generations that were slaves and now protect us from the ancestral realm.

Perspective: It took the United States less than 100 years to legalize and strip away the right of women to determine whether or not to bring a physical being into the world.

Perspective: Travel delays are experienced as though the wait is 100 years long. The combination of privilege, expectation, and entitlement creates the false reality of suffering and the feeling of 100 years.

Context is critical. The 100 years of work, for myself, a black mother, a black lesbian, a black lover, a black friend, a black PERSON is first and forever shaped by the women in the world who can describe self-define across any/all of these descriptors.

Hail Mary.

De'Amon Harges

My grandfather was a lover of learning, but he didn't like school. I guess he passed along his love of learning to me.

When he was twelve, just going into middle school, he lived in Rutherford, Tennessee, and his father worked on the railroad for half a penny a week, under duress.

Big Mama worked in the cotton fields of Tennessee and all the kids also worked in the cotton fields. It was hard, back-breaking work for a little bit of money. It was always said that education was the way out of this environment.

My grandfather was excited to go to the segregated school. The school he said was "in the backwoods." The journey to school was a twelve-mile bus ride. And even though the schools were segregated, white children and Black children rode the bus together to go to their schools.

My grandfather would take his Bible, which was his main source of reading. And he talked about the amazing Black women he had as his teachers.

One late fall day Granddad was on the bus going home. It was really dark. In the country they had no street lights, pitch Black. The Black kids sat in the back and the white kids in the front. My grandfather, because he was fairer complexioned, would ride close to the middle of the bus.

One night on the way home, a young white man who sat right in front of my grandfather pulled the pigtail of the young white girl in front of him. The young white man blamed it on my grandfather. They were only a mile from the school. The white bus driver stopped the bus and kicked my grandfather off the bus. My grandfather, he told us, was terrified that he would be lynched. Imagine a twelve-year-old Black boy in the 1930s kicked off the bus, eleven miles from home, in the pitch dark. My grandfather was terrified; he didn't know who would stop and see him.

His mother, Big Mama, was sure he was dead or something bad had happened.

After he'd walked for a while, two white men in a pickup truck stopped and asked him "Boy, where are you going?" When he told them, they let him jump in the back of the pick-up and they drove him home.

As they pulled up outside his home, Big Mama ran outside with the shotgun and greeted the men. As they walked through the door, she turned to my grandfather and said, "You can't go back to school. This is too dangerous for you. We want you back in the cotton fields."

Every time my grandfather shared this story he burst into tears. It was a sign it wasn't just about the system holding him and others like him back. It was the audacity that a system would try to stop people from dreaming, in the home of the not-so-free, and land of the brave.

Though my grandfather never graduated from the eighth grade, he was a scholar—a scholar of the gospel, the equal of any sociologist, and professor in the highest university; his wisdom rang supreme. Granddad made sure all his children and grandchildren had rich environments in which to learn. And he taught us in ways that no system could steal from us or block us from receiving.

Grades were not as important as using your imagination, and being curious and kind to others. Failing wasn't an option if it led to learning.

We are writing this book for our ancestors who broke barriers, despite the law and practices they grew up around. They did what was right and just, they protected and loved one another.

Our ancestors have taught us to break barriers and protect and love one another. We are writing this book for the scholars of the fields, the scholars of Big Mama's kitchen. We are writing this book standing on the shoulders of these giants, leaders of humanity—people like Sam Cooke, my mother Shar Baby, poets like Mari Evans.

We dare to learn and be inspired for those who look to the stars for inspiration, those who write new songs for our future, the poets who spin new webs of language and love.

Seana Murphy

In 1965, a woman whom I love dearly was sexually assaulted by the son of her mother's white employer. She was fifteen. As a result, she was impregnated and gave birth to the child at age sixteen. Due to her race, marital status, gender, and class, she was removed from her all-Black school and sent "away." She was forced out of leadership positions in the church youth group because of "her sin."

She is now in her seventies and loves her son. She did not share his birth story for more than fifty years. Her spirit, her body, her mind carry the scars. Each memory relived is experienced as more than 100 years. The work for her is to love. She loves hard, she loves deeply, and she is still healing the scars.

CHAPTER 1

The Original Roving Listener

De'Amon Harges

The epigenetics of belonging in a Beloved Community

In a TED talk, journalist Johann Hari drew on Dr. Bruce Alexander's Rat Park experiments to challenge what we think we know about addiction. In the original experiment, a rat was placed alone in a barren cage with two water bottles: plain water and water laced with heroin. The rat chose the heroin again and again, until it died. Dr. Alexander redesigned the experiment. He placed rats in a park with other rats, toys, and a place to play. They almost never touched the drug water. The difference was not the drug. The difference was the environment. The first rat was isolated. The second had friendship and meaning. This research teaches us to pay attention to what surrounds a person, not just what is inside them. It teaches us to look for abundance rather than assume the inevitability of scarcity. Dr. Alexander's work invites us to pay deep attention to the epigenetics of belonging rather than the epigenetics of isolation.

In 2017, as part of a continued practice of mine, I took a learning journey with my friends Mike Mather, Phil Amerson (retired president of Garrett Evangelical Theological Seminary in Chicago), and John McKnight (cofounder of the Asset-Based Community Development Institute). We visited the east end of Vancouver, British Columbia. We were there to learn from an organizer named Anne Livingston, who organized drug users to use their gifts. They created a neighborhood association called VANDU (The Vancouver Area Network of Drug Users). Anne was a single mother who cared about community. Vancouver was on the verge of a public health crisis because of the opioid epidemic. The city was dealing with an overwhelming number of drug overdoses. Law enforcement could not stop the poppies being smuggled in from Afghanistan or the fentanyl that arrived from the coast of China. They were also experiencing a crisis in affordable housing that left people on the streets. The first day, we spent time getting settled into our hotel, owned by indigenous Canadians.

The next day, we had a lot to see. Our first stop was with the former mayor and now harm reduction leader, Sam Sullivan. While eating lunch, Sam discussed with us that the morality issue was that some people in different social classes get treated differently from those in lower social classes. We met Ann Livingston. She reminded me of a young activist grandmother. She had lots of spunk and fire. She was a single mother who deeply cares for her community. She walked us around the east end of Vancouver, pushing a shopping cart. As we moved through alleys and streets, we noticed the alleys were full of people. Young people. Some were wearing yellow vests, others were hanging out. Some were using drugs. When we turned the corner on the first alley we were at a needle exchange, and we stayed and visited with the people there. It was as pleasant and normal a conversation as you can imagine at a coffee break in any office building.

Ann led us into an alley, which had a canvas covering to keep the sun's rays out. There were tables in the alley where people were playing cards, eating, and writing letters. And while they were doing that they were smoking crack and shooting heroin. One side of the alley had a trailer with a sign that said, "Don't use alone." We asked, "Why is that sign there?" Ann explained: "Most people die in single-occupancy rooms because there is no one there to revive them. When we started making sure people did not use alone, our overdoses went down." Shortly after she explains this, right in front of us, a young man overdosed, and his co-user pulled out Narcan and immediately revived him.

I know it seems like a backward approach. But the other approach, telling people not to use drugs, didn't save people's lives. Ann's cart was definitely like a bag of potion and in it she had Narcan and clothing. But one of the most amazing things is she reaches under her cart, opens up a container, and it has cases of strawberries. She started dishing strawberries out, and I remember Mike Mather asking, "Why do you carry strawberries?" Ann calmly says, "No one ever gives us strawberries."

At that moment, it made me think of the struggles of addiction in my family. It made me reflect how often I have seen my parents in their addiction alone, not known for their gifts, only for their failures, which had transferred to me. This story is a deep and hopeful reminder: cultivating a fabric of belonging leads to joy. It leads people to recognize that they are children of God because they have gifts. The problem is that we assume some people must first be healed before they can contribute. They already do contribute. We simply miss it. Because of what Anne and her neighbors had done—turning a public health crisis on its head—the overdoses drastically went down, because the gifts of the residents in the east end of Vancouver were recognized and were able to be contributors to the solution to the problems that affected them the most.

Four Ingredients in a Beloved Community

1. There must be a fabric that cultivates abundance and possibilities.

2. People's gifts must be recognized and used in the community.

3. They must be celebrated in the common good.

4. Social fabric must make room for the stranger.

We aren't here to build community, we are here to remember it!

In 2012, I was hired to go to Thunder Bay, Ontario, to conduct a training on asset-based community development (ABCD). I was there with another friend and mentor from the faculty of the ABCD institute. We co-led the training that was a day-long event. That morning, before the training started, an elder from one of the indigenous tribes, the Anishinaabe in the province of Ontario, was there to help us set context for the day. He started out by sharing the gifts and history of their culture—his story—and stating that every human is important along with the gifts they have to give. He then went on to say, **"We aren't here to build community, we are here to remember it!"** This is asset-based community development at its core.

ABCD isn't something that was created. It is something that happens all the time. At the same time that scarcity is taking place. It is a stance and a practice of noticing what is right in front of us; the beauty that surrounds us all the time. It is based on abundance, possibility, and faith. The elder in Thunder Bay stated that community is already happening. Our job is to simply be present and notice where abundance is happening. It challenges us to look deeper into each individual and see them as if they were children of God.

Oftentimes I am in conversations with people who work in the social services, or nonprofits and philanthropy. All seem to want quick fixes and sometimes look at asset-based community development as a monolith for an answer. They often say, "Yeah, we know about asset-based community development. It's about finding the needs of the community." This is not what ABCD is about. It is about the relationship of abundance with people, our ecology. That is intertwined with the stories of the past and the present. Asset-based community development is about equity, sharing what we have, and noticing the opportunity for people to be in relationship with one another and this planet. When I first met my friend Mike Mather, he didn't start with my problems. He didn't ask what it would take for me to get my diploma because I didn't graduate from high school. His first question was about the circumstances of my birth. There were no social service agency, church, or other helping agencies that I know of that start with that question.

Our birth stories are doorways to our gifts

While reflecting on my time on this planet, I can't help remembering the experiences inside the margins of 100 years that have shaped me and the practices living in a beloved community. My birth story is an important story. It isn't the story that just belongs to me—I can go back over 100 years and it would tell you the story of why I do, why I am, and who I am a part of. My story is wrapped up as not just me overcoming barriers but it is shaped by a fabric of love—which means I get to share what is poured into me. I get to remember what abundance really is, especially when things get hard, and I give thanks to my parents.

I was born to Deamon Lewis Harges and Sharon Yvonne Braylock. They met in middle school through my uncle, my mom's younger brother Aleck Braylock Jr., who was my dad's best friend in elementary school.

Mom and Dad were both creative. They both came from hard times in different ways. My dad grew up with a single mother. His dad passed away by the time he was ten years old. He was one of five kids, with three older sisters and one younger brother. Dad was very good with words, very charismatic, very nurturing. He was an activist and somewhat of an idealist with an imagination that was bigger than the universe. He adopted my grandfather, my mother's dad. They had a lot in common. They both loved music, learning new things, and they are good teachers.

My mother was very shy. Yet was one of the best performers I ever knew. Her charisma would light up a room when she performed, and after she would perform, she would go back into her shell. She was very introspective. Definitely a collection of her parents. My mother was a storyteller, a musician, and a visual artist. She definitely loved the place she grew up, and the way she learned life lessons was through remembering the community, just like the elders in Thunder Bay.

Their shared creativity led my parents to date and eventually fall in love with each other. I remember my mom telling me that she loved my dad because she saw and loved his creativity, and my dad really enjoyed the way my mom expressed herself freely. He saw that she was not afraid to express herself. This opened up the activist inside him. He believed in justice, but my mom was his inspiration to act on it. Between them, they loved sharing their gifts with each other. They both had skills and wisdom they brought from their ancestors. My mom taught my dad how to play guitar, as she did several of the young men in high school and around South Bend, Indiana. They were not only boyfriend and girlfriend in high school, but they also became bandmates. Music and dreaming became part of their lives. Their relationship became a doorway to the currency of imagination. This imagination is the foundation of my birth. I was born out of love and joy.

Eventually, they started a family. They both had high hopes for their children's futures and wanted us to dream big, despite our circumstances. So with the intention of bringing greatness into the world, my dad dropped out of his last year of high school and got a really good job at a factory. My mom started out working at Sears until she got pregnant with me. In 1973, this was a hopeful time. My dad purchased their first home shortly after I was born. He had a good-paying job at AM General, and my mother was able to stay home, at least for a little while. My dad started out working on an assembly line, helping to assemble and test drive military vehicles. It was very hard work, but he was proud of it, and he was proud to be a dad.

My parents had the highest hopes for me. My sister Barbara was born in 1974, ten months after me. In fifteen months, in May 1976, my brother Andy was born. Our parents loved us with all they had. My dad picked up a double shift, and my mother would double down helping us get through our first year of elementary school. Because we were so close in age, my siblings and I became best friends, like teammates. Since I was the oldest, I was the leader, even though my sister was known to be a little more responsible than me. My brother was the funny one, always full of humor and laughter, especially in hard times.

Pain, an instrument of imagination

The 1980s became the age of awareness for me. It's where I learned that some people have means and some people don't. Some people are allowed to have power and some people's power is stripped away, and some people are just plain invisible. I was seven years old, just leaving the first grade. I remember this time being close to the end of sitcoms like *Three's Company*, *Sanford and Son*, and *Chico and the Man*. It was the age of the modern world. Shows like *Miami Vice* and *The A-Team* featured Black actors like Philip Michael Thomas and Mr. T. It was the age, the revival of young people pushing back. We were using our creativity to become visible. It was the early days of the era of the computer and only a little later, what would become "social media."

I remember my parents crying after Reagan won the presidency. Of course, I didn't understand why but their tears told me it was important. I soon learned it was not good news for Black people in the country and in South Bend, Indiana. I struggled in school, but I love school. I would always get in trouble with my teacher because I couldn't read.

I would get embarrassed because I struggled to read out loud. Later I would find out I had dyslexia and probably ADHD. I was sent to the remedial classes, and I struggled to read.

I wanted to be in the group for the top readers. Those kids were really smart. I started to dream: What could I be? I wanted to be a teacher like my grandfather. I want to be a poet like my dad. I want to be an artist like my mother.

My sister and brother both struggled in school and this would shape my own lack of confidence. My parents seemed a bit worn out by day-today life and felt less engaged. They always watched the nightly news and had opinions about how the world should work.

My dad was a former activist and protester interested in social justice but now worked for "the man." My mother used her skills to educate us in painting and music. She would use her art to tell the story about individuals in our community and their gifts.

Grandma called out to each of us when we are growing up. At first, she would dream big for us and when she asked us what we wanted to do, we all said we wanted to be doctors and lawyers. That is what our school told us we should be.

Deep in my heart, I knew being a doctor was not for me. Being a lawyer? Not interested. I was pushed to see that was my only future. My favorite subjects as a child were history and social studies. I knew all fifty states and their capitals. But I was a dreamer— but not only a dreamer for myself. I wanted to dream for and with others.

By 1983, I am twelve years old and in the sixth grade. I am discovering hip-hop: Kurtis Blow, Grandmaster Flash, a little later KRS-One of Boogie Down Productions, and Public Enemy.

Two years earlier, the assassination of Anwar Sadat, a peacemaker, hit me hard even at a young age. My parents were devastated. They looked at Sadat as another Black hero, slain for trying to bring peace.

Because my parents were raising us, they had no time to do the organizing and dreaming work that they'd done in their youth. My mom picked up a job because my dad was laid off. It was around this time that I saw what it meant to be Black and treated differently. I knew this because I had money that was colorful—we knew them as food stamps—and it was embarrassing to hold the money that wasn't really money.

The crack epidemic was raging all around us. My dad thought he could make some extra money by engaging in that sort of entrepreneurship. My mother would try to get assistance from the Center Township Trustees, but would often come back empty-handed.

I felt defeated because I watched my heroes, my parents, finding no way out. My dad would self-medicate, first with beer and at times I would smell the aroma of marijuana. I started giving up in school because it seemed like other kids were doing better than us.

I'm going to school with hand-me-downs from my grandparents taking us to Goodwill. We were often laughed at. I became angry.

I would sit up at night, knowing that my parents not only were struggling to keep food on the table and keeping bills paid but there was less attention spent on telling us what we could be.

Though they were picking up extra work, my parents still found time to be together. They still played music. There was a band almost every weekend at my house and we were center stage. My father found solace in music and would often play rebel music like Bob Marley and Stevie Wonder.

On the weekends we were sent to my grandparents, which was respite for them and respite for us.

Our grandparents found time to instill confidence and creativity in us. This is when Grandad, who was without work, was a teacher to his grandchildren. He would sit us down and tell us stories and make us toys, and soon we learned to tell our own stories as he created. We would often hear the story of "the Learning Tree." And he would read scripture to us just like he did with his neighbors when my mother was a child. He made me feel alive, like I could be anything I wanted. And all I wanted was to be just like him.

My dad went back to work, but he was still attached to the entrepreneurial spirit of the crack game. He started drinking more and went to rehab a few times. I noticed that my mother became more anxious, no doubt caused by tension between her and my dad. When we came home from school, she would be waiting for us with a hot meal made from ingredients from the food pantry down the street.

She would tell us stories from our youth. She would name the people in our community, then she would put out a drawing pad and draw them.

As we got to know these stories, we started telling stories ourselves, and she would draw those too.

At the age of twelve I discovered a few things about myself that hadn't occurred to me before. I felt more responsible for contributing in my community and in my family. I felt if I got a job things would be better, and I got my first job as a paper boy. I had tried shoveling snow, and cutting grass, which was all good—but a working as a paper boy was a legitimate job.

My route was in my own neighborhood, so I got to know my neighbors. I loved it when people would be good hosts and offer me a tip, some candy, or share a short story with me about people in my community who knew my parents.

Some went to high school with my parents, like my wrestling coach Carl Evans. And it wasn't just old classmates who knew them—it was the shop owners too. My mother would often send me with a note to the Kolocz brothers, the local butchers, or to Kuburski's, the local bakery, and Starlight Pizza. I never looked at the note, but I knew that my parents didn't have money and they were asking for groceries on credit. This lack of money humbled us, but it also provided us an imagination for how to cultivate trusted relationships. I don't know if my parents ever paid off their credit at these shops, but the store owners knew my parents by name and I knew they trusted my parents. They had created currency in the community of trust. This is how I first learned about social capital!

My ancestors' generations passed down to me the value of being a good neighbor. These values were my own parents' practices pouring into me even then.

Later on, I was able to use those learnings as an entrepreneur myself. I often heard that "it takes money to make money," but what I witnessed was that it took currency like trust, love, history, and relationships to make money.

It took a little bit of trying, creativity, and imagination to make things work around my house. I am learning to become an entrepreneur. I also took the lesson of paying attention deeply. I may not have had the best grades, but I was one of the best listeners. If you didn't have money, being a good listener makes you able to spot an opportunity as it arises.

Being an entrepreneur requires being a good listener, being quick on your feet and full of imagination. I must admit my journey to entrepreneurship started out a little rocky: shoveling snow on school days off turned out to be a disaster. South Bend is known for the huge amount of lake effect snow, with piles like felt like mountains a hundred feet tall. Even if they were only twelve feet tall, it was overwhelming. I took my only loan out and borrowed my parents' shovel. I remember when my dad left for work and he asked us not to go outside, but the snow was too tempting. My sister and brother urged me not to do. I said, "Don't worry about it. I'll make some money." I broke his commandment.

I took my snowshoes and snow pants, put them on, and took the shovel and walked up and down our neighborhood. All along the way I saw friends along the way having fun. The distraction was too much for me; I ended up playing football in the snow.

I got home after my dad returned from work . . . and he was furious. I only made two dollars. That was the day I learned that failure was also part of entrepreneurship. Over the years I took that lesson, and I'm a better entrepreneur now because of it.

My parents eventually divorced, and I became the breadwinner. I got better at cutting grass and my paper route was semi-successful. I had a summer job, but I also started learning to cut hair. I was doing it because my parents didn't have the money to get our hair cut, so I learned how instead. Hip-hop influences meant my haircuts were modeled on the flashy, big hairdos of the Tribe Called Quest and Big Daddy. It turned out that practicing on my brother was good advertising: neighborhood kids would see my creative designs and want their own.

I hear stories all the time of how people grew up, and I think about how I was cutting hair on my own by the time I was fourteen. I would have twenty to thirty people on my mother's front porch at a time all waiting in line to get a haircut.

The stories I would hear while cutting hair lit me up. I think I enjoyed it more than making the money. That storytelling experience only made me want to create more avenues for people to engage one another. My neighborhood had a fantastic dance culture, and I began creating a dance contest, sometimes spontaneously. I would also organize a rap contest. Also known as a cipher with breakout, it is a contest to see who can use words in the most creative way possible, producing the strongest metaphors and best stories in only sixteen bars.

People enjoyed the atmosphere, and I actually made some money. Because I was so shy, my mother was always surprised at how many people would hear about my work and want to hang out on our porch.

Our porch was the gathering space. One day, my mother walked outside, really excited to see all the young people there. She looked at me and said, "You are an entrepreneur."

It was the first time I had heard that word and I didn't know what it meant. She would also follow up and say "June, you like the Pied Piper." I didn't really know what she meant by that, either—but I would come to find out.

By the time I was seventeen, I felt like I was always fighting for my life: fighting to have a place in this world, and fighting to have meaning. A lot of my friends had passed away or were facing prison sentences because of the crack epidemic. In high school I fell in love with wrestling. I thought my only card left to play was to be an Olympic wrestler after the season was over, but my final season was over long before that—because of my grades.

So I dropped out of high school at the age of seventeen. I was two credits short, but couldn't muster the energy to overcome the grief surrounding me. I worked three jobs: Steak 'n Shake, Olive Garden, and in an apartment complex. I also started dabbling in the arts, doodling and writing poetry.

At twenty-one I moved to Chicago, to West Garfield, also known as K-Town, a community whose story was shaped by gang activity, heroin, and crack. My great uncle was a longtime resident in this neighborhood. Part of me wasn't fazed by the harsh realities there, but other parts of me knew that things could be better. To cope with all of this, I started diving into poetry more deeply. I would go to a place called Africa West, which was very near the old Chicago Bulls stadium, where I reconnected with my ancestors. I got to be around other creators—barbers, visual artists, authors, and other entrepreneurs—who talked about why things were the way they were.

This place had my type of vibe. The poetry I heard moved me and made me feel alive. I started getting on the train and writing and writing, watching people and writing about the things I saw and learned along the way.

It was then that I knew that creativity and artistry were part of my call. I would spend years in Chicago learning the streets and people in the streets and they became my teachers. I was learning the conditions Black people lived in weren't a punishment from God but a response to what a system allows communities to respond to. I would hear Dr. Paul Farmer later say: "We have been schooled in scarcity."

Now I was all grown up with a head full of dreadlocks and fire in my belly that kept my smile radiant as the sun. I now realize that I'm in charge of my own destiny. It felt like being born again in 1999.

I moved back to South Bend. My mother lived downtown and there was an apartment open. I got a job at a coffee shop called "Higher Grounds." I realized that I love working in the public and my whole aim wasn't to serve people coffee, but to get to know people's stories. I took my entrepreneurial spirit and my stylish, creative love for words and started an open mic gathering at the coffee shop.

The open mic was called "The Collective." We met on Tuesday nights and it was packed just like my younger years. I was good at bringing people together. I realize that it was what my parents and grandparents did and I was doing it to heal.

I also had a part-time gig as an AmeriCorps Volunteer at the Life Treatment Center (an addiction support program) on the southeast side. I attended to people who struggled with addiction, people like my parents and neighbors, people like the ones I knew from my childhood—people who were always more than their addiction. I would get in trouble for getting personal with these people, because I wanted to know their stories. I just kept sitting down and doing art with them.

I would often talk with a young white woman who worked with me. Even though I was known to be a troublemaker at the center, she was more interested in my gifts for art and working with others.

One day she came in and told me that I needed to meet this pastor she knew. He was the pastor of Broadway Christian Parish, which was right down the street on the corner of Carroll and Broadway. It was a tiny congregation down the street from my cousin's house. I actually didn't know much about that side of town, except the local gang and that it was our red-light district.

I have to be honest: I wasn't looking forward to meeting the pastor. I didn't believe church made a difference. I kept thinking, "What's a pastor gonna do with an artist?"

After a shift at the center, I finally worked up the nerve and went down to the church. I was a little disappointed because the pastor was on sabbatical and wouldn't be back for another month, but I met a woman named Becki, who worked as a community builder (her job title was "Animator of the Spirit").

I thought that Becki's job was interesting, mainly because it seemed to have little to do with church. As I knew it, she started telling me about the pastor's philosophy and what her job was in the community. It was hard for me to grasp. I think it was hard for Becki to grasp. It sounded like this pastor was a hoot, maybe a little off his rocker. But I have to say that meeting Katie was like a thing that was supposed to happen.

I learned that Katie's mother was the parish nurse at the church.

It turned out that Becki was really good friends with my mother when she worked for the city. My mother was shocked when I'd met Becki and she knew who I was. I started going every day to hang out with Becki. She would give me some odd jobs and made sure that I was able to meet the pastor when he got back. Now, meeting (the pastor) Mike for the first time was a little awkward. My first thought was that he was going to try to baptize me or get rid of my heathen ways, but it turned out he was like no other pastor I'd ever met. He was very casual, very disarming and his office was filled up with piles of books towering over him. I remember sitting in his office and within the first few minutes of sitting down, he caught my attention. He asked me about my story, where I grew up, and about my parents and my grandparents.

I kind of thought I might have been in trouble for something that I may or may not have done, but as we get into the conversation more, this white dude earned my respect. He wasn't like most white predators who preyed on the lack in people. He wasn't like any other social service agency that made a living off of people's pain. He genuinely wanted to see me and in return, I would take the journey with him.

After telling him my story of growing up in South Bend, I told him about my open mic at Higher Grounds. I told him that I was into hip-hop and how much Public Enemy inspired me to think about justice. I said "Mike, do you know the song 'Black Steel in the Hour of Chaos'? It's one of my favorite songs."

He reaches behind his chair and pulls out a Public Enemy album. This white dude was cool, and I was hooked.

He knew he had me also, because community was my thing. He shared with me his philosophy of community. It was the first time I had a sense of being in the world, and I was able to see a world bigger than myself.

When Becki left her job at the church, Mike offered me her position. Mike was excited that I accepted, and I was excited both to try something new and not give up my open mic or my job at the coffee shop.

I became a community arts coordinator. When I took the position they called me "the roving artist." My job was to take a backpack full of art materials and drop them off to other artists in the community on the southeast side. Barely twenty-six, here I with the power to be a contributor—this time not just for my family, but for other people in the community, people who were first strangers and who later became friends.

The church became a canvas for young people not being seen or feeling seen. Young people tagged the church, leaving images on the brick and showing off their skills for storytelling. The church members were a little concerned that there was graffiti on the backside of their church and that they couldn't catch who was doing it.

One day I was walking to the church and I saw fifteen- and sixteen-year-old people tagging the church. I walked up to this very diverse group of young people, led by Nick, who happened to live right behind the church. They were a little startled, and I convinced them that they weren't in trouble. In fact, I really wanted to get to know them.

I went back to tell Mike that I found the artists using the church as a canvas. He had given me money to paint the playground equipment a couple months back. I had to admit I was a little behind, but at that moment I told Mike that I'd found the folks who were responsible for the graffiti. He asked me, "So what do you wanna do about it?" and I said to him that I wanted to hire them—and I did.

Now Mike was interesting, because he always seemed to look at things through an abundance lens, that there's always the possibility of taking a bad thing and turning it toward something good.

I got close to Nick and the rest of the artists, and I learned that they felt unseen. They were happy to help me paint the playground equipment, and as we were almost finished, Mike introduced me to Bill, the curator at the South Bend Regional Museum of Art.

Bill has a very gentle and generative soul. He came at my request to talk about an exhibition on the Holocaust. He got to see some of our art laying around the church and invited us to lead a community exhibition. We were shocked (in a good way), and we couldn't believe our ears and eyes. He invited us all to come down to see the space at the museum and he offered us unlimited art supplies. I saw in him an artist just like my own grandfather, turning seemingly nothing into something of beauty.

Now we had another problem: All of the young people who were in the artist group had gotten into trouble and were sentenced to spend time at the juvenile justice center. I told Bill, "If this is gonna work, you have to write a note." We had three months to prepare for this exhibition with a theme of "holocausts." We told Bill we didn't think we could do this. We didn't know anything about the Holocaust. He turned around and said, "I think you do. You all have a holocaust of y'all's own." Needless to say, the exhibition was successful, with close to a thousand people at the exhibition's opening.

Not only did we participate, we designed the whole gathering. We had a rock band, a hip-hop band, and we performed poetry together. It was the first time that I've seen the work of my grandparents come to fruition breaking barriers—as young people, as artists, as people often overlooked. It was the first time that any of us had ever been into a museum, and to be a part of something so big with so many people attending. It was one big place full of love and joy! I was starting to find my own way. It was the first time I felt what the spotlight is like and what it means to be seen as a creative servant leader, to belong and to be regarded as a contributor.

In discovering my own gifts, I began to discover others' gifts. And my budding friendship with Mike became more than just a pastor/parishioner relationship. We became friends, kids in the playground pursuing wandering joy. It would lead to a quarter century of discovery and impact. The white dude and I would become social inventors together.

I eventually landed a job in Chicago as a first-grade teacher's aide and later became a teacher. In 2001, right before moving to Chicago, I went to New York City on a learning journey with young people from the parish. That trip would become a practice that has shaped my life ever since. The learning journey expanded my world even more as I traveled with other young people to see exciting and inventive ways to be community. We went to New Jersey to see the New Community Corporation, which was spearheaded by MacArthur Fellow Monsignor Bill Lindner and led by Black residents of Newark, using their gifts and talents.

I was inspired because there were people who look like me with the imagination to see the systemic barriers as just a stepping stone. It was surely an abundant land. We also went to the South Bronx to visit a place called The Point, a community organization in the belly of Hunts Point also known for a thick Latino culture and creativity, who also did not allow systematic racism to limit them. They were God's people.

Now I'm back to reality. I'm in Chicago the day after I moved and started my new job at Alain Locke Academy, a new charter school on the west side. I was walking distance from my great-uncle Peter's house. I would walk proudly to work with kindergartners and first graders. I thought about what my gifts offered me. I get to teach young people in the shape of the future because that's what great education is for. Frustration wasn't far ahead. I quickly discovered the struggle of teaching had nothing to do with the students being difficult or with Black parents not being able to teach their children. The rules were too one-sided, unable to handle complexity. Schools seemed more like warehouses for servant leaders to simply remain servants. I felt the weight of being Black and poor and working in a system of scarcity that wanted me to be nothing more than the custodian of the poverty. I didn't want any of that.

Still, I found hope in this madness, hope for myself that I was able to teach even though I didn't have my own high school diploma. It was social capital that built these trusted relationships, just as my parents and grandparents had in their community. That was the currency that led me to use my gifts. I was known as "Mr. D," one of only three Blak male teachers in the school. Most of the students lived in a two-mile radius of the school.

There was a young man in my afterschool program named McKeith, a second grader who was playful and curious. He was full of wonder and he would change my life. He introduced me to his mother. It was a rocky start; do not mess with mothers and their children! She was not happy that I didn't let her son go to the bathroom right before the bell rang, and I explained to her how overwhelming the afterschool program was. She didn't buy it. For the next few weeks I would give her a cold stare, thinking of words that were not exactly Christian.

Eventually, the ice broke, and McKeith's mom and I started dating. Janeen became my wife and fellow sojourner in cultivating a beloved community. Within months, our daughter, DeJanea, was born. My children are now thirty-one and twenty-three; one is a biologist who plays with molecules and the younger moves molecules in community.

So now with a teacher shortage in Chicago Public Schools, pressure to keep teachers is mounting. The inertia of poverty in a school of scarcity felt like ten elephants on the teachers' shoulders. I become a first-grade teacher, which seemed like an achievement to me. We had a new principal who was a former lawyer, and her job was to get people through the rigorous testing that the state required. She was no-nonsense and had a good heart for the work. She followed the rules and did everything right—which is what she thought had gotten her through, and what we all thought would get us through. That would backfire on me, because I love to break rules, especially the ones that aren't right.

In the play *Gem of the Ocean*, August Wilson wrote of a shaman woman defending a man unjustly accused of murder. He describes a moment when she was met by law enforcement, a Black law enforcement officer, who said they had to take the man in. She held up the bill of sale for her person, issued more than a half century before, showing that she had been a slave, and she said to the sheriff, "Just because you have a piece of paper and it's legal doesn't make it right." I think people in my community have always lived by that same logic.

The gang activity on the west side was heavy. It seemed to provide a sense of meaning to many young Black men. We were told statistics say that by the time these young men were in the fourth grade, they were tasked to make a decision about gang life. A gang was where people saw your gifts. At school they only saw you as a body and a number to take tests to get funding for the school. I admire my cousins and neighbors who were in gangs not because of the crimes they committed or the fights and violence they inflicted on the community. I admired them because they did what a system couldn't do—they made a place where people belong, a place where your gifts were needed and valued and rewarded.

The school had no tolerance for weapons. That made sense—except that a community not seen will always find a way to make its own rules. When creativity is suppressed by the relentless demand for test scores, the zero-tolerance policy grows more and more absurd. The tools of creativity get reclassified as weapons. Just like in prison.

One day, a young man brought a box cutter to school because it was part of his science project. One of the kids made a big deal that it was a weapon, and I heard about this and went to retrieve the box cutter. I called his mother and I told my team teacher, who told the principal. I ended up in trouble because I had aided this young man with a weapon. Even though I would not change what I'd done, I was fired. I told the principal that I would not have changed my decision, and it didn't quite add up, that the whole situation was an unholy act. I was devastated. All my hopes and dreams went out of the window.

At this point I began losing hope because the systems of scarcity were drowning out any sense of abundance. The abundant hope of my grandparents, the hope of my parents, the hope of all those parents, Black faces in a Black neighborhood—it all felt like it was slipping away.

One of the few things that gave me hope in that season was my friendship with Mike. He drove straight up from South Bend to Chicago to see me. He consoled me and reminded me that my gifts were still needed. We talked about continuing our work together, dreaming out loud about what that might look like—neither of us knowing that the next chapter would find us on our own playground, walking and playing and dreaming. That is what led me to my true calling as the original roving listener.

The Original Roving Listener

In 2003, the kids were one and eight, and Janeen's job at the railroad transferred us. They closed down the Chicago office and gave us a choice to move either to Philadelphia or to Riverside, California, both far away from our home and our families in the Midwest. Both places were very expensive and because I wasn't viable on a job market even with all my experience, I could not make the money to keep us afloat. Janeen's salary was not enough to sustain us even with her benefits. She also respected my friendship with Mike and knew that he was becoming a big part of our lives. Mike and I always talked about getting together again in South Bend, but that never happened because he moved to Indianapolis. Six months later, the pieces fell into place. Through a connection in the neighborhood near Broadway United Methodist Church—where Mike served as pastor, a congregation he had first come to as an associate pastor—we learned there was reason to come to Indianapolis. Janeen's job was offering her a transfer. Our eyes lit up. We rented a tiny two-bedroom apartment where I would commit to being a stay-at-home dad while Jeanine went to work. Our kids shared a bedroom on Broadway in the neighborhood called Mapleton Fall Creek, so much like the neighborhood I lived in in Chicago. It had the reputation of a not-so-good place. The community didn't have a lot of money, and they were known for police runs and a lot of violence.

I started to see a pattern, but I also saw an opportunity. I would come tell Mike stories about what people were doing. I talked about possibility, imagination, and people using their gifts. I continued that practice every week. I would walk up and down the streets with my daughter, DJ, on my back, and I would tell Mike stories about what I saw.

It was an alternative story, because the story was about a young Black dad who looked like me being a teacher to not only his children, but other children in the community. The community was full of healers, storytellers, artists, and growers of fresh vegetables and fruits.

Earlier I used the term "custodians of poverty." When I think about the neighborhood in Indianapolis, I think about the nonprofit system that knowingly and unknowingly served as custodians of poverty. These custodians are very good at educating people around scarcity. But no one benefits from that education, and when I started attending Broadway (in Indianapolis), I realized just how true that was.

We kind of went along with the program offered by the nonprofit systems around us, hoping to feel good about ourselves. My own paradigm shifted too because even though I grew up in those systems, I had bought into the hype. In my gut, I knew something wasn't right. My congregation knew something wasn't right. The people in the neighborhood also knew something wasn't right, but what could you do about it?

Mike took this struggle to shift the paradigms seriously. As a pastor, his role went beyond the pulpit out past the walls of the church, starting with wrestling with an old summer program. His most challenging teacher through all of this work was Seana Murphy. Seana's reputation preceded her and will last long after we are dead and gone. I first saw Seana was in worship at church. It was clear there was fire in her belly (more like molten lava) with a touch of love and grace. She grew up in that neighborhood around the church and grew up in the programs, but she was also a leader in the neighborhood and remains one still.

If anybody can change a system, it is Seana. When I first met her, she was running the 21st Century Scholars program for the state of Indiana. Later she worked as an educator designing systems where young people could thrive—especially inside models of scarcity. For Seana, family always comes first, and that lens opened up my own. Many of her neighbors became my teachers too. They helped me see through new eyes: that a community's fabric, though complex and sometimes painful, is also soulful, and that imagination is one of the most powerful currencies it holds.

Some of those families had been rooted in that pocket of the neighborhood for decades. The Buddhas were the largest—most people assumed they were a gang, but they were a family, one of the biggest around. The Evans family was the second largest, living within a one-block radius of the church. Walking down to visit Mike during after-school hours, I'd pass their houses and slowly begin to understand what it meant to have that kind of staying power in a place.

I would often see young people playing football. The families were like teams. There were the O'Bannons. The head coach was Nora O'Bannon—the grandmother. Sierra was about thirteen, Montell about ten. My first real encounter with Sierra was on the field. She would play with all the boys and beat them all.

One time I had a run-in with Sierra; she and a friend were working on a project, and Sierra wasn't shy about letting me know what she thought. She could really talk some smack. But that run-in led me to Mrs. O'Bannon, her grandmother. Mrs. O'Bannon stood over six feet tall and had a presence that was stern but kind. She became one of my closest neighbors and friends.

The Evans family—siblings and cousins—all lived within a block radius of one another. You would've thought they owned that block. And they kinda did. They were always out on the porches. Their household leadership was matriarchal, plain and simple: two sisters. I came to know Carmen well. She had three children, the loudest voice, and the best smile in the neighborhood. Carmen is excellent at math. She threw great parties and gatherings, especially for young people, and worked in the church's summer program—the program Mike writes about in "Having Nothing, Possessing Everything."

Though a single mom, Carmen was always there for other mothers in the community. Trienna Evans, the shyer of the two sisters, had four boys and one girl—the girl was the youngest, and a twin. My first real connection in the family was with Sean, an athlete and a serious button football player who, like any teenager, had his challenges. Sean was respected by a lot of the young men around there. He had real leadership in him. He was also warm, easy with a smile; he got that from his mother, Trienna. Sean would often get kicked out of the house for spats between mom and son.

Eventually Sean ended up at my house a lot, and sometimes I would walk him back home to help broker a peaceful reunion. I was usually introduced as the guy from down the street. Walking into that house felt like walking into a full roster—people everywhere, the whole place full of joy and love. The two youngest were Jalen and Jada. They were about four years old at the time. They were in their own world, playing. I don't think they even noticed me.

A few years later, those two youngest would become my teachers. I had no idea what Trina and Carmen thought of me when I walked in, but I found out later: they thought I was homeless and felt sorry for me and my daughter. I guess I had that look—like someone who felt lost. Little did I know they'd help me find my way.

Every day the sun was out, I would walk the neighborhood. Almost all the young people were out—football, basketball, hoop dreams, scholarship visions. I could picture the uncles and aunties who put those dreams there: old stories dropped into young hearts, giving hope inside a system that didn't give much in return.

Among those out there were also children under eight—including the youngest of the Evans family. On my walks down to the church, my daughter, DJ, came with me, riding in a pouch on my back.

She was just two years old, but she had the eyes and the soul of an eighty-year-old. I think people respected seeing a dad out there with his kid; I'd always get stopped, people asking about her. It gave me a good excuse to be curious.

For the next several months from fall 2003 up until the following year, the Broadway congregation thought about their role in this Black community and what it means to be a good neighbor with a longtime mission statement of "seek, welcome, and value all people." The congregation wanted to know if they actually practiced it and did they have evidence of it. Around the same time the neighborhood development corporation was exploring some of the same questions. The executive director of the development corporation was a member of our congregation and historically there was always a member of the church on the board.

The development corporation invited our congregation to be part of the strategic plan. They wanted us as partners.

I was still continuing to talk with Mike about the people I was meeting—and what if people in our neighborhood knew how powerful they were? What if they could share their gifts beyond going to a program, beyond waiting for someone to come help them?

Mike was getting some good ideas out of our conversations. He knew I wasn't too keen on administrative work. I never wanted to fill out time cards. I wanted freedom to explore. Some people would say I was unsupervisable. Mike is kind of the same way. We had a lot in common. But we never directly talked about it as a few more months went by.

Mike told me the development corporation was doing a strategic plan based on the gifts, talents, dreams and passions of our neighbors. The corporation asked me, How would I like to get paid for what I already do? I was thinking, How does that work? But I didn't ask what he meant.

Mike said, What if you continue discovering the gifts, talents, dreams, and passions of everyone in our community, and then tell the development corporation—and the church—about what you discover? Keep celebrating those gifts and find spaces for them to be used in ways that build up community, economy, and mutual delight.

It was the first time that I heard my parents' and my grandparents' gifts and learning wrapped into a job description.

Since the development corporation paid half my salary, they wanted to be in charge of supervising. Mike knew that was going to be impossible. He knew they didn't really understand what it meant to build on the gifts of neighbors rather than their needs. Mike also knew I had a creative spirit and struggled to conform to rules.

This would change how people would know me.

The corporation wanted me to pass flyers out about meetings and tell people how much they needed to be fixed. But one of the best institution-building acts I've ever witnessed was Mike using his power to give me freedom. He told the development corporation he would put up half the money if they would let him supervise the position. That was to hold firm on why we were there in the first place—making clear that this work is about shifting the paradigm of who's valuable and who has gifts.

Systems of scarcity have the magnetism of a Black hole. They hide the gifts, the knowledge, the wisdom of the community. Mike, just like the first time I met him, had faith in my gifts. What I lacked was also very visible—but he chose to lead with what I had. I formally got the title: the roving listener.

My daily task was to go door-to-door, block by block. Listen to everyone in the household, from the youngest to the oldestl discover what they were good at; what brought them alive; and who walked alongside them on their journey. In other words: who loved them.

I kinda lost sight of my own natural gift. I started being formal, creating a survey with formal questions. The first few weeks, people would look at me like I was crazy. I thought something was wrong with me, like this whole idea wasn't working. I couldn't figure out who to say I worked for—either way, I got the door slammed in my face. If I said I was from the church, they would start telling me what they thought I wanted to hear; and if I wasn't giving out things, they seemed uninterested.

If I said I was from the development corporation, the door got slammed even harder. The residents had been treated for so long as if they had nothing, could do nothing, needed to be fixed. And our church had been part of that—for decades, we'd helped set up those conditions, keeping people from giving their gifts in ways that could have changed all of us. We thought we had the answers, so we built all those cute programs.

No wonder no one believed we actually wanted to see them—really see them. I kept telling Mike the stories I was finding, but I didn't realize the gift I was already using: paying attention. After a few weeks and a little nudging from Mike, I went back out without the clipboard. I stopped asking questions and just started paying attention.

Miss Anita lived catacorner from the church, and I talked with her almost every day. One afternoon she asked me to come over and help take out some trash. Her granddaughter was home sick from school. After I brought the trash down, Miss Anita offered me a drink.

Her granddaughter brought me a piece of pie, called me Mr. D, and said, "I think I know what you're looking for." I ate the pie. It was delicious. Then Miss Anita started telling me stories about how she sold pies to churches in the area during the holidays. You could feel it: this was her gift. The pie was good, but the joy she had talking about it was even better.

This was when I realized that the lessons I'd been learning as a child—about deep listening and entrepreneurship—were coming to fruition. There were other discoveries too, like how many gardens were in the neighborhood, but there were already a lot of gardening programs. There were over forty-five gardeners in a four-block radius around the church. But the development corporation was running a gardening program with fewer than ten people in it.

These programs showed the lack of imagination and scarcity we had been practicing. We had failed to see the gold mine that those forty-five gardeners represented, but we had to go look deeper and pay attention to where people were spending their time.

Those gardens were in the backyards. The only way to find them was to walk through the alleyways.

I met people like Miss Rose, who had been gardening since she could walk. She became a grandmother at a young age. She talked about how gardening saved her life. And Ms. Jackson—a healer in our community, with green beans climbing up the front porch to shade the people who came to visit her.

There were many other discoveries that became surprising. It also becamemiss frustrating because people had all these gifts and were using them and yet were unseen.

To relieve the frustration there were a few things I learned: never ask for someone's gift if you don't intend to utilize their gift in the life of the community. The other I learned a long time ago during my first learning journey to New York City: When you feel stuck, take a journey to give you a little bit of imagination and possibly connect with people along the way.

A friend and guide for me at the time was my friend Mike Green, who was part of the ABCD Institute. He was introduced to me about a year into the project via Mike Mather.

Mike Mather suggested I take a trip with Mike Green to the Adirondacks, where Mike Green was gathering with five other community builders to rest and share their work. Mather thought it would help since the work I was doing felt kinda lonely. Community development work is usually focused on what people don't have, so when I came back with stories about all these beautiful and holy things people were doing, nobody seemed to believe me.

I also struggled with the fact that I was supposed to write reports. The reports were important; the church and the development corporation wanted to know what I was finding. But I didn't really understand what reporting meant. I also have to admit that my dyslexia took over so I needed to figure that out as Mike Green and I arrived at the small gathering in the Adirondacks. There were five wise guys sitting around a table. They greeted me and all knew about the work that I was doing.

Three immediately became mentors. Jack Pierpoint is the founder of the Inclusion Press out of Toronto and the convener of the Toronto Summer Institute every year. Jack is a social innovator and champions the rights of low-income communities, indigenous communities, and communities with disabilities. The cocreator of the Toronto Summer Institute, John O'Brien, who is a renowned conscientious objector, college president, and champion of the lives of people with disabilities living full lives, using their gifts in community. John McKnight, who was a legend to me, was cofounder of the Asset-Based Community Development Institute, then at Northwestern University. I was telling them about the things I was going through and needed some advice. It was great. It was Jack who became instrumental in my understanding my need for other people.

Jack said to me: One of the issues you're having is that you're doing this alone. Who can you take with you? He suggested I find seven people around me who could listen. John suggested that instead of writing reports, I find someone to transcribe for me—and told me his own first books had been transcribed that way.

I went back home with a renewed sense of direction. I started asking church members to come along with me. I needed other witnesses to what this work was about. That helped build and connect community.

Having Mike as my supervisor was an advantage. He understood something about my disability. He also knew how important it was that I actually be out there listening — not behind a desk. He saw me in action, even when I didn't realize it.

Mike gave me some extra money to hire one of my neighbors to transcribe. Then a friend and church member who lived in the 'hood—he was finishing up his master's in social work—offered to help.

He created a data report out of my stories. I started out telling the stories of each house and address about everybody in the house. I did this for each block for about a five-block radius around Broadway.

In nine months there was a report called "The Roving Listener." On the front page it asked, Who is your neighbor?

The report noted how many pairs of shoes I wore out in those nine months, how many people I talked to, and what gifts were discovered in the blocks I covered. It was powerful. And it tested our partner institutions: They wanted the data, but when they got it, they couldn't figure out what to do with it. They never did.

I also used these visits to connect people. Each week, there was a gathering at the homes of those I'd visited.

We did not hold these gatherings at the church. The church was seen as having all the power partly because we acted like we had all the power. In fact, the church was nicknamed the White House, no pun intended. There was always a host on each block—someone everybody knew. I would invite the people I'd met on that block, and then invite our partner institutions too, but with some ground rules since they were used to running meetings.

Their job was not to ask questions but to listen. It was not to tell people what plans they have but to listen to what people are doing.

My first few gatherings, people were a little shy. After the third meeting, we went back to Miss Anita's (who was a beautiful host) and we met with about twenty residents. The dining room was packed. There was so much excitement.

A young man, Brandon, who was a photographer had heard about the meeting. He brought his whole portfolio. It became a conversation about celebrating folks with pictures. The development corporation heard about this and lit up. They asked for me to bring Brandon to a development corporation meeting.

Brandon's story was featured in the report, but it made a difference. Seeing him face-to-face, in fact, made the institutions around our neighborhood curious and I became a broker for the talent that was already there. Brandon made friends in the room that night.

At the same time, Broadway was working on a new infrastructure that would let the church actually receive the gifts of its neighbors and begin living into its mission statement. Members of the church were energized. The days of living with nostalgia were coming to an end.

Well, not really an end. There were still funerals to hold for the days gone by. One of the things we had to grieve was the belief that we were the answers—that people only needed us. What we replaced that with was the understanding that every person in our community is needed.

We used worship time to grieve those deaths first—to begin creating the fabric we needed. Once a quarter, we would say together "well done, good and faithful servant" to each thing that was already dead that we'd been pretending was still alive. It was like a *Weekend at Bernie's* moment, honestly. We also recognized we needed a space for people to share their testimonies in real time. We added a moment in worship and called it "The Lesson from the Contemporary Church." Because God didn't stop writing when the book went to press.

This practice was the beginning: The gifts that were already visible to me and my community started to become visible to others.

The testimonies named and celebrated what people walked past every day without seeing. They gave everyone who wanted it a reason to be a good neighbor—a kind of mutual delight. This practice became meaningful in ways we hadn't expected: threads finding other threads, slowly weaving together a fabric of joy and love.

CHAPTER 2

Work and Money

Michael Mather

You can hear in De'Amon's story the sense of wonder, imagination, and joy that flowed through a very different path than mine. De'Amon certainly did not shy away from the hardships he bore witness to in his family's life and in the life of the community in which he grew up. What comes through most powerfully is the joy, from his grandparents and his ancestors and his community.

Visiting a new doctor recently, I had to give a family history. Why? Because the history guides the doctor in understanding who you are and what she should be paying attention to moving forward.

I hear people in communities and congregations I have served often say, "Well my family may have held people in slavery, but I didn't." Yes, true. But our history helps us know what troubles are gnawing at us, what opportunities for growth might have smooth sailing, and how we might all be healthier and wiser and more full of joy. We are all connected, after all.

The epigenetics of joy moves through my bones and my bloodstream. It has found me living and working in communities most looked down upon and despised and thought of as nothing. Yet what I discovered there was something I didn't know I was looking for: joy. And my history delivered it to me. And my friends have helped me to see it when I was blind.

When I was a child, I was enchanted with money. I knew we didn't have much. How did I know it? Because the answer every time I asked, "Can I buy that?" was "We can't afford it." It's the way I remember it. Money seemed powerful. I had seen it bring my strong mother to tears when she didn't have enough money to buy us shoes. If it could bring the most powerful person I knew to tears, then it had to be amazing.

Money seemed powerful when the most respected people in the church took the responsibility to collect the offering from the gathered congregation. The whole congregation would stand and sing together as the money was carried to the front and reverently laid on the altar. Then the pastor would pray a prayer. No wonder I thought money was important and powerful.

I've thought a lot about money and power as I've lived and worked at the intersection of poverty and wealth my whole professional life. While living and working in communities defined as "poor," I came to know the wonders of a neighborhood where a world-renowned poet had put down roots—because the house was big enough to hold all her books. Where a musician and inventor put a hydroponic garden in his backyard and a recording studio in his basement. Where people would come from around the country to participate in pop-up concerts in the basement of a seemingly quiet house on the block.

Yet everyone called this a "poor" neighborhood.

One constant through the years has been thinking about the relationship of money and power in this country and in the institutions with which I've worked and struggled with and against. Noticing people's power and pointing it out to others and trying to understand its relationship to money, even investing in unseen/unnoticed power, is 100 years work.

My dad grew up on a farm. Strawberries, lambs, cows, and corn. They didn't have a lot of money, but they had very good food. My mother's father died when she was five years old. She and her mother survived by repairing and making clothes. Mom remembered sitting next to her mom on the sewing bench as grandma sang, "A Bird in a Gilded Cage."

The ballroom was filled with fashion's throng,
It shone with a thousand lights
And there was a woman who passed along,
The fairest of all the sights
A girl to her lover then softly sighed,
There's riches at her command,
But she married for wealth, not for love he cried,
Though she lives in a mansion grand.

She's only a bird in a gilded cage,
A beautiful sight to see.
You may think she's happy and free from care,
She's not, though she seems to be,
'Tis sad when you think of her wasted life,
For youth cannot mate with age,
And her beauty was sold,
for an old man's gold.
She's a bird in a gilded cage.

My grandmother felt like a bird in a gilded cage. My mom's experience growing up fed a great anxiety about money. She carried that anxiety throughout her life.

Where we come from matters.

One Sunday morning after worship, a recently retired white couple asked if they could talk with me later that day. During worship a Black city council person told the story of housing discrimination in our city and in the nation. The councilor described the loans to and investment in the white middle class (and in some cases lower class) persons through the 1950s and 1960s and beyond. These were investments and loans and tax breaks that allowed (mainly) white folks to build wealth while their siblings of color did not have that same encouragement, investment, and actual dollars.

The white couple on Sunday afternoon told me they were giving me $20,000 because "our parents, our families, benefited from this" and could I put this $20,000 into the hands of low-income, low-wealth Black people from our neighborhood? They didn't want the person(s) to know who gave it and they didn't want me to tell them who got it or in what ways it would be used. These were not wealthy people themselves, but certainly solidly middle class. They would know they had $20,000 less once they sent the check.

What to do? No seminary class had prepared me for this (why not?). No college class had prepared me. No conversations about this ever appeared in my preparations for ordination in the church I have served for my whole professional life. I had to completely make it up.

I thought let's give large sums ($1,000-4,000) to a variety of neighbors doing good work among their neighbors. $3,000 would go to a couple who were building a hydroponic garden in their backyard. Another $2,000 would go to a neighbor who was always willing to fix his neighbors' cars (for free) and who spent time with young people at the local high school who were autistic and from his neighborhood.

Each would be surprised to get these gifts. And while I would not tell them where this money came from, I would tell them about the intention behind it. Then I thought about it some more. Why was I doing this so I could get all the thanks and compliments? Well, the truth is I like getting thanks and compliments, but I needed to step back.

De'Amon's work as the Roving Listener expanded into other neighborhoods, other places around the country (and the globe). He had worked with young people from the neighborhood and walked alongside them as they met their neighbors discovering the treasure among their neighbors. This went on for several years and the young people were now leading this work.

They had years now of finding out the gifts, talents, dreams, and passions of their neighbors (old and young). Why shouldn't *they* get the thanks and compliments? It was because of what these young people learned about the gifts of our neighbors that brought these folks to our attention.

I loved to hear their stories of the giftedness of our neighbors. I loved the questions the young people developed, on their own, to really find out how these persons gave themselves to the world.

They asked questions like "What are you most proud of in your life?" "What do you love about this neighborhood (a place where people had been conditioned and encouraged to talk about in the worst possible ways)?" These young people shone like the sun with what they heard. Why, why, why should they not be the ones who get the credit? It wasn't my money.

I met with these young people from our neighborhood who were meeting their neighbors and I told them the money was theirs to distribute to celebrate people who were making a contribution to the life of their neighborhood.

Those young people now have a different story to tell. I wonder how they will tell it twenty-five, fifty, or more years from now? Will they tell of their agency and power? Will they tell a story of white guilt and paltry repentance?

Or will they remember it as something inevitable. "If we are learning the gifts of our neighbors, *of course* people will want to invest in those gifts. And when I have some money, this is what I'm going to do with it!"

My privilege, my whiteness, gave me power to share. It wasn't anything I earned. It wasn't anything I deserved. It wasn't the way I had been taught by the church or by society. It was a way to do something consistent with how my neighbors treated one another. Recognizing gifts, celebrating the gifts of my neighbors, gave room to create space where investment could happen. Investment taught me what my role as pastor is, and to understand how the church could act (and does act, at its best). Rather than be the delivery vehicle of services, what if the church is the place where people are recognized for their power, come together to dream about how to act on that power, and then find social capital, including friends, who want to support them in their ventures?

Creating space, creating sacred space where possibilities can be imagined is holy work. "Look at what you can see all around this neighborhood!" Some investments worked. Some didn't. And when we failed and when we succeeded we learned and it fed ideas about what to do next.

I remember decades before, a wise mentor, saying to me, "If you are going to be paternalistic, go all the way."

At the time, I didn't understand.

Later I came to believe and acknowledge my white privilege and paternalism, not deny it, and use it in ways I couldn't imagine before. It was good to see young people giving out this money and *not* telling people that it came from someone at the church, but it had come from the young person and their friends. Beautiful. Where had I learned this? Many places—that wise mentor for one.

Another was from Seana when she was a young adult. When she was still in her late teens or early twenties, I watched her one day on the church steps.

Three siblings between the ages of four and eight were hanging around talking with Seana. The youngest asked if Seana had any money. Seana reached into her pocket and pulled out some change. She turned to the oldest and gave him a dime for his youngest sibling and told him to get something for him at "Frog's Records and Tapes" around the corner. Seana gave him another dime and told him to buy something for the middle brother. Seana then handed him a quarter and told him it was to get something for himself, and that it was more because he was taking responsibility for his brothers.

She had recognized her power, she had shared it in a way by telling those three boys she recognized their power and they belonged to one another. They felt powerful. They are powerful, she reminded them. It was a mirror they looked in and liked what they saw.

I didn't like to admit money was powerful. Yet it is. Even in my own discipline I know the Bible has a lot more to say about money and the lack thereof—exponentially more—than it has to say about anything concerning sexuality and doctrine.

The church has money (even when it is not very much money). How we spend it, how we disburse it, says as much about our mission or more than any program we are supporting reveals. Is money going into the hands of people who are poor (who don't have money)? Are the people who are benefiting from whatever this action is intimately involved in the planning and delivery of this product/service/idea?

These were never markers for me along the way. Until I began to see it through my neighbor's eyes. When I sat in their homes and listened to their stories about everyday life and navigating the systems allegedly supporting them. Now I had alternative stories to help me understand the world.

It's pretty easy to see. Money comes through "serving institutions" and is dispersed in services to the poor. This was how I had operated as a pastor in low-income, low-wealth communities.

Decades ago, folks at Northwestern University told me about a study on poverty back in the 1960s and 1970s that reported there was $6,000 per person in poverty coming into Chicago in the early 1970s. If you gave a family of four $24,000 during those years they wouldn't be poor anymore! Instead, only less than a quarter of that money actually went to the family. The rest was rendered in "services."

I received money from grants and donations and then I provided service and sometimes cash in small bits (usually for "emergency assistance," which were constant emergencies). I learned from the culture around me a lot better than I learned from paying attention to the people I was allegedly "serving." I had never even tried to figure out before whether what we were doing was actually working. Twenty years after I became a pastor and we started moving the money directly into the hands of the poor we ended up having more positive effect on people's economic status, health, and levels of joy (or what we call "mutual delight").

This is still true. A colleague did a study a few years ago where she wrote to religious institutions in Indianapolis asking them what they were doing with regards to working with persons and families in poverty. She followed up with the ones who responded and asked them, "So is what you are doing effective?" No one answered with "yes." The answers were mostly "I don't know" or "we hope so."

When we started investing in the gifts of our neighbors, other stories were being told. Those stories gave people eyes to continue imagining new ways of being, acting, doing.

How this will play out fifty years from now, or 100 years from now, I don't know. I do know these new stories will shape a future I do not yet see, and will probably never see. I feel much better about it now than if I were still doing what I had been doing at the beginning of my work.

When I began to treat our neighbors as if they had agency, gifts, and power, this confused other organizations.

I see this playing out today in the same ways. When I suggest investing in people who live in the streets, I have had people write, as one person did a few weeks ago: "Rev. Mike, instead of hiring someone who lives on the streets to identify the gifts of people who live on the streets, we have excellent programs in Boulder. Maybe we should invest in those . . . by the way, things have gotten worse and worse in Boulder around this issue."

So what could we do? We believed profoundly and deeply in the gifts, dreams, talents, and passions of the people around us. What would allow others to see this?

We decided to hire two people who live on the street and call them "Illuminators." What is their job? To identify those gifts, talents, dreams, and passions and then to share them in as many places as we can imagine. We have had them meet with the church council. We have had them meet with the Personnel Committee. We are working to have them sit down with the chamber of commerce. The Illuminators are giving them information that they would not have. They are opening blind eyes, if the people on the chamber and beyond will take a look. The Illuminators have even been invited to a communications class at the University of Colorado to talk with them about how they use digital media in sharing the word, in creating safe space, and in sharing their gifts in the community.

People have stopped me when I've been out in the community and asked, "Are you the pastor at the church who has hired people who live on the street?" Then they want to know what we are learning. We don't know what will come from this, it's new for us, but people are beginning to believe there is giftedness in unexpected places, simply because we invested in investigating this!

In the mid-2010s I was asked by the leader of a neighborhood not-for-profit what we (at the church) expected from our neighbors.

Out of that conversation and conversations with laypeople at the church, one of the principles we put forward was "money flows into the hands of our neighbors." This is what is known as a policy decision. If money came to us for work in the neighborhood, the money would go into the hands of the people it was alleged to serve.

I've received a lot of pushback about this across the years. People will say, "You can't give poor people money." And I understand what they are thinking even when they say, "Poor people will spend it badly." I know, I spend money badly! I imagine you do too. I don't spend money only on things that are healthy and good investments. I try . . . most of the time.

If you are poor you don't have a lot of room, a lot of money, to make mistakes, especially if you spend it unwisely. Even if you are acting philanthropically: lending to a friend, a family member, a neighbor, you're often in worse shape. Some argue doing things this way won't change things. They are thinking short term. I know because it was how I was thinking. I'm someone who paid people's "emergency" bills for a lot of years. It didn't solve things in the short term or the long term. Showing people that you trust them, even when mistakes are made, grows roots that can blossom in the future.

By changing our practices, we have rebuilt atrophied muscles in our organizations. That atrophy has kept us from seeing the people we serve as gifted, creative, entrepreneurial, generous people. When those things are invisible, they do not receive investment. When they are revealed, it gives people the chance to invest in and encourage those gifts.

I learned this lesson in a very surprising way in 2019. I got a call from someone who had read my previous book, *Having Nothing, Possessing Everything*. This person was calling from her job at a large corporation, asking if I could talk with her about poverty. After an hour-long conversation she asked if I could be a consultant on poverty to the corporation where she worked.

I said no.

"Why not?" the person asked.

"Because a consultant is a thing and I have a thing. I'm a pastor."

The person asked if we could continue our conversation about poverty occasionally. This was something I could do. Six months later the corporation gathered several of us together to talk every week about ending poverty. While I thought it strange that a corporation would be having this conversation, I was game, particularly because they were committed to involving people who are poor in the conversation. Early in these conversations, the corporate leaders brought up the subject of most effective means for bringing people out of poverty. Several of us whom they had gathered said it was fairly clear to us "money" is what gets people out of poverty.

The corporation executives were a little thrown off by this. They had hired researchers and they turned to the researchers who confirmed this was the most effective tool. The company said, "Well, maybe we need to do more research." The researchers said, "You can. But *all* the research says that this is the most effective way."

The company representatives answered, "Well, we can't do that." "Why not?" we shot back.

"Because," they said, "we don't trust people."

Yes! Stating this truth was actually helpful. Then we could talk about developing strategies to address the real issues, which were far more about trust than anything else. How do we invite people into relationship with one another so that currencies of trust, as De'Amon called them in the last chapter, can be built?

One of the answers we developed was to invest in the projects/programs/ideas generated by people in low-income, low-wealth communities. Once we began to think this way, the possibilities bubbled over. As we invest in people in low-income, low-wealth communities, the word goes out that "we have good ideas" and "other people believe in us and what we have to offer." This is exactly what builds trust.

In the first conversation with the people with the corporation, De'Amon asked all the people in the conversation how they got their jobs. Each person told stories about relationships with friends or family members, or someone connected to them, giving them their first jobs.

Training programs can do a little bit to help. Yet it is the relationships that are the most important characteristic.

When I prepare for funeral services, I hear the stories of the person who has died, including stories of how the person came to their lifelong work. Almost always those stories involved an important person in their life opening a door.

100 years work takes building relationships; it takes tearing down the walls, and it doesn't happen overnight. Trust is not developed on a spreadsheet. It takes time, intention, and a willingness to fail. It also takes people, leaders at all levels, to be creative and courageous in how to change these long-term dynamics militating against change.

I was talking with a colleague about their work with a large not-for-profit in the Indianapolis area. They had not been successful in hiring a diverse workforce. Why?

When they were searching for a new employee, the person getting the job was almost always someone they had already known, and the white folks employed at the company only had relationships with other white people. If their workforce was going to look different they had to cultivate more diverse relationships in their private lives. Relationships have economic impacts.

The company worked on practices, like having social events, where diverse peoples were invited to meet and, as De'Amon says, "fall in love with each other."

Hiring practices began to change. And as more people of color were hired there were more people who knew candidates who were low income as well as people of color. This change begins to build new economic futures. This seemingly small shift is how transformation actually works. This is how it has always worked. The issue is opening up the possibilities to people who have been blocked.

While it happens at the level of large corporations, it also happens at the neighborhood level.

De'Amon was telling me about his conversations with his neighbors. He had been noticing how much money changed hands between people and households in the neighborhood. Some of these households were related to one another and some were not. De'Amon had invited some of his neighbors to begin cataloging how much money passed between hands in the neighborhood. It was a lot. People helped one another pay bills—rent, utilities, food, school costs, and more.

All of us writing this book have at one time or another both supported and been supported by, economically, people we know and love. Did it always go smoothly? No. But we made our way through it. And it continued. Doing things the old way didn't always go smoothly either.

Poverty doesn't mean "no money." The poor don't have much money. They do have some money. Poverty is also traumatic. Poverty is also neglect, piled upon neglect. It has 100 years, 200 years, 300 years, 400 years and more of weariness, a poison in the body, as Seana has made so very clear.

If it is to be rebuilt, if healing is to happen, money is part of the solution. So is recognizing the costs of pain and misery and incarceration and anxiety piled on top and on top and on top.

We were trying to do what Seana wrote about in the introduction about the epigenetics of joy. Celebrating the gifts of people, believing people have joy, means finding practical and practiced ways to live out these gifts.

100 year work is looking ahead. Making investment where there has been disinvestment. Reimagining what investment means, what it looks

like, how it's measured as a way of recognizing the myriad of ways that this happened long before the concept was created and implemented.

Looking at people as wondrous rather than wicked, as marvelous not just manic, as purposeful not putrid, is centrally important. People have literally turned their noses up at people who come in to my church without a place to wash up and get clean and without a change of clothes that allows them to clean when they are living in a tent (or not) along Boulder Creek. The poor are looked down upon by those whose ancestors washed their clothes in the very same creek! Poverty is turning away from people and literally not seeing them.

100 year work starts with paying attention.

Maybe Mary Oliver's instructions on living are most important for the dominant culture in this society, for 100 year work: "Pay attention. Be Astonished. Tell about it."[1]

Too often, we avoid paying attention so we run programs providing the services we believe people need. All while keeping people at arm's length. One of the ways we are encouraged in this by our society is when people who are poor or hurting come to us we are encouraged to "refer" people to helping institutions. "Referring" people means we are walking away, or sending someone away who has given us the gift of encountering them.

Every third Sunday of the month at my church in Boulder we provide a free lunch to anyone who wants to come. One of the oddest things I heard from some old-timers is that we are only "supposed" to feed people who can't afford a meal.

In other words, people who don't have money and people who do have money are encouraged (*mandated* even, by one of the places the church gets the food from) not to eat together. And whether this is a rule or a guideline, it is certainly a narrative providing an escape route to anyone who doesn't want to have to encounter someone who is poor.

In conversations we have about this around the church, one of the people in our congregation pointed out the people who come to the meal are a gift to us. They aren't getting a whole lot of nutrition out of one meal a month from us.

On the other hand, we have the opportunity, the gift, to get to know people whom we otherwise would not know, and learn what a treasure chest they are for our larger community.

If we don't eat together, where will we learn the stories, the creativity, the talents of the people we encounter? One person told me he had met a guy who lives on the street who has a master's degree in classical trombone from the University of Texas. People are endlessly fascinating. Every single person and discovering them more deeply is the very thing improving our odds at becoming a better, healthier, more just society.

We have a young woman in our congregation who was born with Down syndrome. Evie recently graduated from high school. She loves music and fantasy stories, and all the things a teenager usually loves.

When Evie was eleven she decided to get into politics, hyper-local politics. She ran for student council at Louisville Elementary School.

Then it turned out she would have to give a speech! She paused, thought about it, and then said, "I'll do it."

She worked on her speech:

> Good morning. I am Evie Larson. I am running for Student Council. I help my friends.
> I help my friends when they are sad.
> I help my friends when their feelings are hurt.
> Please vote for me.
> Thank you.

When it was time to give the speech, she was nervous. Her teacher asked if she wanted help. She nodded, and pointed to one of her competitors, Bella. Bella read Evie's speech, and Evie turned the pages. Evie didn't win the election.

It was close: fifteen votes for Bella; fifteen votes for Cooper; and fourteen votes for Evie.

She lost by one vote.

And it was, remarkably, hers.

Each person could vote for two people. She wrote Bella and Cooper—her friends. When asked why she did that, she explained, "They are really nice."

And so is Evie—who helps her friends. As her dad Chris says, "Now that's a campaign we can believe in." Evie teaches us this: everyone has something to teach.

When we label people, we miss all this person has to teach us.

When we treat people like they are needy rather than needed, we all end up poorer for it.

Power and agency are denied the poor, but are present in every choice they make, even the ones that don't have a variety of options available. Power is made perfect in options. The difference between people without money and people with money is people with money are perceived as those with options, with agency, with choice, with power. People who are poor have choices as well. Fewer certainly and a bandwidth that doesn't stretch too far.

I visited an economist, Eldar Shafir, at Princeton University. He said, as he did in the book *Scarcity: Why Having Too Little Means So Much*, that the problem with anti-poverty programs is not user error; it is a design error.

Over coffee he told me about fighter planes crashing when they were landing in World War II. They retrained pilots, but the planes kept crashing. Then they noticed some very similar planes were not crashing. Why not? They discovered the planes not crashing had the landing gear button and another important control on opposite sides of the cockpit. The planes that were crashing had them right next to each other. It wasn't pilot error; it was design error.

We have designed our solutions without taking into account the abilities, passions, and commitments of the very people we are trying to serve.

The design error here is there is *no* button for people's gifts. So the button can't be pushed. The capability is there, but the knowledge of it is not. These are not poor people's errors; this is design error. And we can fix it. It won't be easy. We'll make mistakes, but we can fix it.

Beginning to see the poor as people who are amazing because they know what to do when they have been evicted, when the electricity is turned off, when the water isn't running is not about glorifying their resilience, but instead acknowledging all that should be honored: the intelligence, and resourcefulness at play in their lives every day in ways that those who have more options cannot fathom.

We use words like *resilience* in talking about poor people in a way we don't often use with those who have more money. We call people who aren't poor "creative" and "smart," not "resilient."

There is a coffee shop recently opened near my church in Boulder. They call themselves a "human rights campaign disguised as a coffee shop." They hire people who are labeled as having intellectual disabilities. They know these folks are needed not needy. What if churches were freedom and joy parties disguised as churches? What if homeless centers were maker's spaces disguised as homeless centers? What if our homes were places of welcome and great food disguised as homes?

Social service needs to turn itself on its head. Churches, religious institutions, government and other serving organizations have an opportunity to determine that the work ahead for us isn't about them and their magnificent generosity, but about their willingness to invest in and support the long-term lives of those they call siblings, but whom they treat as servants.

If we can recognize the poor have developed good strategies for sharing money that helps keep the heat on, maybe they can be put in charge of the distribution of so-called "emergency assistance" (hard to call it that when life is constantly an emergency). If we recognize everyone as needed and not needy, then justice systems can become places not of punishment, nor even of rehabilitation, but of restoring people as community healers and gift givers and citizens.

Years ago, De'Amon held an event on his block he mentioned called the "Cultivating Joy Cypher." It was a place where young Black men in his neighborhood were celebrated and recognized. What also happened at this gathering was communal grieving. It didn't take the full weight of the universe to pull it off. Only some neighbors willing to take a few minutes to come outside and celebrate their sons, partners, fathers, spouses, neighbors, and friends. We all have a lot to learn from events like this one.

One day I joined De'Amon as he walked down the street with some young women in their early teens. While they walked together, he asked them what was wonderful about their mothers. As they told him what they noticed, they were hearing one another celebrate their mothers.

Sometimes we don't know all we have in our hands. It's a lot, it *really* is—if we have the eyes to see, there is a whole lot to celebrate.

I won't forget stepping in the home of some neighbors who needed help with a utility bill (because they didn't think it's possible that one would invest in their gifts!) and noticing a one-dollar bill taped to the archway that divided the living room.

"What's that?" I asked.

One of the women answered, "We put it up there to remind ourselves that even when there is nothing we still have a little something left."

I learned lessons like this all the time. One of my great teachers is Seana Murphy. Seana sees the world with great clarity. Her description of how the world and its systems work, through her lens and experience, keeps me focused on what joy has to contend with in worlds and systems that only see need and fail to see their contributions to it.

The work of 100 years begins when we learn to ask different questions—not "What do you need?" but "What do you know? What can you do? What do you love?" Work and money are not ends in themselves. They are what happens when people who are truly known bring what they carry into a world that is finally ready to receive it. That is the gift economy. That is the 100 year work.

CHAPTER 3

100 Years Work from the Inside Out

Seana Murphy

According to the Bible, Sarah, mother of Isaac, was ninety years old when she became pregnant. She lived to be one hundred and twenty-seven years old. Abraham lived to be one hundred and seventy-five years old. This longevity matters when we are talking about 100 year work. 100 years work feels chronologically measurable; it is not. Biblical measurements of time demonstrates this. Sarah and Issac's spirits measured how long it took for them to conceive. Our spirits are the real measures of time. My grandmother would measure time against the phrase: "in my lifetime." This is the measurement against which the speed of change must be measured. It is measured against the people doing the work both visible and invisible and those resisting the work and all of the structures in between. The length of time is particularly difficult to measure when attempting to make changes within institutions that benefit from maintaining the status quo (Pimps) and those who have internalized the belief systems perpetuated by the institutions. It is the reinforcement of the belief systems that allow oppressive structures to stand.

Chapter 3

Changing from Inside Out

Pimpin' ain't easy.

Several years ago, I was in a conversation with a community center director who had been awarded a significant amount of money to reduce poverty in the community. When challenged to prove positive outcomes, the director pointed to the number of people who had completed the financial literacy class. When I pushed and asked, "How many are still poor?" the director responded, "I don't know."

I pushed harder, "How many of the two hundred people that came through your program were lifted out of poverty? Ballpark it if you have to!"

The director continued to say that he didn't know. I responded that "according to everything we've seen, these classes do not move people out of poverty. Instead they teach them how to maneuver poverty. So unless you defied the odds, the people are no better off than when they entered your program." The director could neither confirm nor deny. This is Poverty Pimping 101.

A group of people put on yellow vests and walk gentrified streets monthly. They then point to lack of homicides in those strategically selected communities as evidence of their effectiveness. Ignoring the impact of gentrification. Narrowly defining violence as the absence of homicide. Willfully remaining silent around the uncomfortable alliance that is shared between the "watch dog group" and the police. In turn, the group enjoys press coverage that provides the platform needed to reiterate the tired pathologizing and victim blaming narratives that further injure an already harmed community. The curious element of the group's existence is that unlike other donor dependent groups, it is rarely pressed to provide clear evidence of impact. When pressed by the communities that are allegedly "helped" by their presence for concrete evidence of their impact, the leaders fall further into tired troupes by accusing questioners of "doing the white man's bidding" and personal attacks. They are violence pimps.

Pimpin' ain't easy. This phrase should make all bristle. It should also push one to examine the ways in which pimpin is encouraged and celebrated. The fact is that the ways in which people and stories are used to leverage money and power mirrors the end goal of any pimp; to exploit, control, and have material gain. .

Throughout the course of my work in the community, I have listened to institutional leaders justify the claim that "without us, these people will perish" and "the need for (fill in the blank) narrative" by pointing to the questions and requirements of funders. The leaders allege that funders will not fund them unless they are addressing a need. I struggle to believe the narrative. I have met sophisticated funders who understand the complexities of community. Funders who seek NOT to help but to encourage organizations to do innovative-life affirming work in spaces that are unfairly categorized as "deficient." Unfortunately, the number of funders working from this space are overshadowed by those that are "need based" and "need driven."

Need based and need driven approaches are dangerous and gross. Several years ago I served on a grant review committee. A white, female led, organization applied for funds to support counseling for young black female victims of sexual assault. The application detailed the stories and the number of young black girls/women who were victims of sexual assault. As part of the application, the woman went into great details about the experiences of the young girls/women in the community. As part of the narrative, she implicated fathers, boyfriends, uncles, brothers (every male gendered identify available). The narrative was heart wrenching by design. Committee members shook their heads, some teared up, while reading the narrative. I was outraged!

My outrage stemmed from the fact that this white woman took liberties in pimping the stories of these young ladies.

I questioned the use of their stories as a means of strengthening the quality of the application. I questioned whether or not anyone else on the committee questioned the use of this type of narrative to move the committee to approve the application. I questioned whether or not these young women would have shared (if they shared in the first place) their stories with this woman if they knew that she would use it as a tool to advance the organization's bottom line. I also questioned the specificity of the perpetrators. Did these young women actually tell her that the perpetrators were relatives and/or their mother's boyfriends, or were these the white woman's embellishments? If the young girls/women were that specific, what did this woman do about it? Where is that part of the narrative? If these things were told to her, why did she position herself as the savior? Where in the narrative is she creating community from within given funding limitations? I further questioned whether or not the seventy percent of funds being used to support existing staff members-would actually have a positive impact on the lives of the young women.

I lost the challenge. This exercise did prove that pimpin' violence against girls ain't easy—but it works. Since that experience, I have participated in convenings with community groups led by expert fundraisers and learned that there is a fundamental lack of imagination regarding what can and cannot be funded. In the conversations, when challenged to imagine a world where funding is rooted in the good that is happening despite the "needs" in the community, the room was stumped. This illustrates the impact of internalizing deficit based narratives-questions around measuring impact arise-as though the impact of investing in joy cannot be measured-it can-people are happier, less isolated, and confident in the strength of their communities and neighbors. It is not hard but requires risk and imagination.

What would it look like if philanthropic and other institutions invested in the joyful aspects that exists in the lives of "those served"? What would it look like if JOY was a treated-in a real way-as a key social determinant of health? What would it look like if funders required joy as a key component of grant applications? What would it look like if institutions across the country (philanthropic, municipal, community) rejected the deficit-based narrative? After all, in the state of Indiana pimping is illegal.

Pimpin' 102: Jesus—or a Reasonable Facsimile—Will Fix It

Karl Marx's claim that religion is the people's opium is often quoted as a critique of those who believe in a higher power. Religion is not inherently addictive. Religion, like any other experiential elixir, becomes addictive when placed in the hands of the powerful and is then monetized and peddled as the antidote to individual suffering.

The pimping of Jesus (speaking from the tradition and experience with which I am most familiar), is the way to isolate and exploit individuals by drawing attention away from systemic issue. Pimpin' Jesus shows up in today's world society in a variety of ways. The Prosperity Gospel and Christian-based programs that require prayer, repentance, and conversion to receive basic living necessities are just two of the most common variations.

Colonialism is a byproduct of the Savior pimp narrative. These are global truths that are very rarely challenged. Pimpin' the Savior is not relegated to white people. Pimpin' the Savior is operative across religious, social, civic, educational, and other capitalist institutions. Pimpin' the Savior requires self-aggrandizing. Heroic stories of the life changing impact of "human service".

These stories reveal the magical superpowers of the institution: a Savior that can sweep in and transform the lives of the people. I was recently in contentious conversations with such Saviors. In each case, the Saviors spoke excitedly about going to other countries to "help" the poor build buildings, plant gardens, educate children. My response to the conversations was catty: "How many buildings will you drive by on your way to the building location? How many trees will you see, how many people selling vegetables will you pass along the way? How many kids will you see playing, smiling, and talking with their friends?"

The questions were asked as a way to highlight that the "help" that was being provided was at best ill informed. If you drive past all these things and the abundance they reveal, then what "help" is really needed? More importantly, how much more "helpful" would it be if you sent the money spent on travel, food, charitable giveaways (why does everyone want to bring crayons, toys and bubbles on these trips?) directly to the organization that has expended time and resources in preparation for your arrival?

HBO's docuseries Savior Complex is a bone chilling example of Savior Pimpology. The white woman in the documentary used the privilege of race and religion to justify abusing Black bodies on the continent of Africa. According to this woman, "God does not call the qualified, God qualifies the called." Emboldened by her faith and her white Jesus, she ran a clinic-conducted medical procedures on Black children, several who were disfigured and died, without any fear of retribution. Where in the white world can any person get away with this behavior in a white community? This woman blogged about how exhausting the work was but save for Jesus, she pressed on. The woman pimped the stories of the families, the illness of the children, and the "lack of resources" to raise money to continue "her work" She, under the guise of Jesus, committed a crime against humanity. Her crime, an egregious example of the Savior as a pimp, is not unlike crimes happening across the global community. She "saw a need" and acted-without conversation, without proper training, without basic decency of disclosing that she had not idea what she was doing. She experimented on black children and was protected because of the "good" that she was doing. Though not as egregious, each time individuals or groups (regardless of race) act on perceived need without first exploring the gifts, talents, and possibilities that exist within the community, a crime against humanity is committed.

The Savior Pimp is a shapeshifter. Sometimes the Savior Pimp appears as the corporate leader that hosts a $100-per-plate fundraiser to announce and celebrate the removal of the box on the application that asks whether or not one is a convicted felon. Removing the box is not bad. However the wealth and power represented in these spaces can be used to challenge the system that over polices communities thus creating a cycle of criminalization that disproportionately affects certain communities. It is the corporation that celebrates itself for establishing training programs in low-income neighborhoods that reward graduates with $15-per-hour jobs while failing to disclose on the front end that the company requires proof of citizenship in order to be hired. It is the Black pastor that demands prayer-touch and agree-before giving a sandwich to an unhoused person.

It is the low-income house complex that offers residents "community nights", access to food pantries and afterschool programs while failing to disclose the relationship between the housing units and the police department that allows for surveillance of residents without their knowledge.

It is the untrained, self-anointed mental health provider that uses the unscientific "tough love" approach to shame and victim-blame residents that are struggling to make sense of the world around them.

It is the dangerous mix of "attitude of gratitude" peddlers coupled with the holders of "The Secret" and the "self-care" gurus who propagandize the "want it bad enough to manifest" and "the love yourself enough" motifs as a way to softly blame communities for the inequities affecting their ability to live into the fullness of life.

When I was in college I railed against the homophobic, racist, sexist practices that were endemic in the systems governing my experience. I did not let an opportunity pass to remind the president of the university of the oppression under which I was required to perform. My consistent pressure eventually led to he and I having a personal conversation where he reminded me that change takes time. My counter argument was that some changes take time—other changes simply require courageous decision-making.

Institutional change requires courageous decision making. The biggest decision that an institution must make is whether or not the practice of pimping is worth it. If the answer is yes, then the institution will move forward under the illusion of change-making and eventually dissolve because "the arc of the moral universe is long, but it bends toward justice."[1] The practice of pimping is an injustice to the community, and though it may take 100 years to dissolve, organizations committed to this will one day implode. (At least this is my prayer).

If the answer is no, then the institution will employ the following practices immediately:

1. **Repent and ask for forgiveness.** This requires a courage that is unfamiliar to most. The courageous part is not in the ask but in being prepared for and accepting of rejection. Before engaging in this practice, you must be prepared to take a tongue lashing as a consequence for your sins and you must be prepared to accept that not everyone will welcome you. The task become taking the time to find those who will welcome and walk along side you in the work. Who are the people that will hold you accountable when you start "back sliding?" Find the people who disagree with your approach but value you as a person. There are lessons to be learned from these people. Finally, remember that repentance is not a one-time event. It is something that happens over and over again. It is something that must be followed up with action.
   Recently a growing number of institutions have adopted statements acknowledging that the land on which the institution stands once belonged to Native Indiana Tribes. Some of the statements go so far as to name the tribes. Some of the institutions offer programming to the descendants of the tribes.
   Not one statement or program goes so far as to say: In acknowledging that we are in possession of stolen land, we are prepared to give it back. Similar to the statements, recent "reparation" acts that have happened across the country acknowledge that the institution benefitted from slave labor. Some institutions offer programs (scholarships, housing grants, etc). This is NOT repentance nor is it reparation. *Repentance requires acting in a different way*. Controlling how the benefits can be used and any other format outside of money is a continuation of paternalism that maintains the power structure and white supremacy.

2. **Start paying people cash** (especially those bound by the ridiculous income requirements of government programs) for their time, talents, and expertise as opposed to the customary mediocre lunch and empty platitudes.

There are so many excuses used to justify not paying people in cash. Those justifications are draped in accounting jargon, moralistic fabrications, and flat-out mistrust of the poor.
These excuses however do not stop institutions from profiting from the wealth of knowledge and experience represented in the viewpoints of the poor. Surveys for example are used across institutions to collect the information needed to determine marketing approaches, increase service, and/or to improve products yet rarely are people paid for the contribution. It is not hard. During the course of 2022, a survey of people living on the Far Eastside of Indianapolis regarding transportation was administered. Each person received $20 for completing the survey.
During the course of surveying, we found that families used the money to take their kids out for dinner, to go skating, and to do other recreational things that the budget did not allow.
It was easy and not one person stated that they were going to go and buy crack cocaine, weed, alcohol, or lottery tickets. In exchange for the $20, the city of Indianapolis learned that the current transportation system is not designed for everyday use. This information was used to shift the public transit routes that allow for more families to access public recreational spaces across the city.

3. **Stop looking down and sitting across from people—literally.**
Physical distance is a display of power. Where one sits, the proximity to another, communicates an understanding of position in the power structure.
Conversations that happen across tables prevents deep connection. I cannot laugh at your joke and touch your shoulders if you are across the table from me. I cannot hold your energy as the table serves as a barrier. When I attend meetings and am drawn to someone sitting across the table from me, I have to make an effort to meet them again, in a more intimate space (coffee or lunch) as a way to get to know the person.

4. **Start building an infrastructure that will outlive your physical presence with the institution.**
Infrastructure cultivation is critical. A lesson that I have learned is that when a strong infrastructure is in place, the

winds of change cannot eliminate the structure. This is important because a strong infrastructure can mitigate the need for 100 years work.

5. **Stop telling stories without the subject's permission.**
Every marketing person knows that before you can publish a picture of an individual you must: (a) inform the person that their image is being recorded and can be used-this is in public spaces, or; (b) have the written consent of the person before using their image in marketing materials.
This same rule should be applied when telling a person's story. The person should be privy to the story that you seek to share and should have final approval of the language. This practice can eliminate the temptation to glorify organizational impact while reducing the individual to the deficiencies that the organization allegedly addressed.

6. **Start creating a culture of life affirming language and storytelling.**
Review materials and eliminate deficient language. Marketing people will not love this idea. This idea pushes you to confront the ways in which the organization has pimped poverty. It also opens the window to creativity while testing the idea that funders and other organizations will refuse to fund unless you engage in poverty pimping. I worked at an organization where I reviewed all publications and eradicated the word need.
Everyone across the organization had a thorough understanding of need. What we did not know was what people were good at, what they enjoyed, and how they could bring those things to bear when working with their children.
It was a culture shift, and it was hard. Replacing need-based language with tips on how to support children in math if you loved cooking, or how to support kids with reading if you loved singing was outside of the established marketing tradition. It was a necessary move. It was necessary because the parents saw themselves as teachers in a way that had been denied them through the need-based language and model.

7. **Stop assuming that people want to be at your table.**
Seats at an existing table are alluring to those who have been denied. There are however people who do not want a seat at the very table from which oppression emanates. Too often, a seat at the power table is performative and there is no intention to listen, hear, and act in different ways. Tokenism is the result and thus invitations are refused or abandoned after injury has happened to the person invited.
Start assuming that there are tables, tents, porches, pews, park benches, etc. where the real work is happening, look for these spaces and ask for an invitation to sit.
Organizations/institutions operate on business hours. The lives of people do not. There are spaces where the real work happens as a natural part of life. Find those places, repent, and ask to be invited as a witness. This will be hard because it will require the parking of ego and voice so that the lessons of WHY and HOW can be learned and internalized. After being in the spaces, give CREDIT to your teachers. Acknowledge that your teachers made you better. Ask your teachers how you can contribute in a meaningful way to the relationship.

8. **Stop handing people paper as a form of intake.**
Paper pushing, be it physical or electronic, is an outdated use of power over and should be avoided at all costs. This is a genteel way of reminding people, at best of the power inequity, and at worst that they are poor and in need. This is unacceptable and not conducive to real change. The "data collection process" in this format is a way of justifying continued poverty pimpin'.

9. **Start collecting information through conversations** (if you are required to collect information for funders-frame the conversation in such a way as to collect the information without reminding people that they are being helped).
Conversations can yield the information needed if you determine that you must collect in-take information. It is a matter of asking engaging questions that affirm the lives of people. Before engaging in the practice however, you must ask yourself, what information is really needed?

Once you deduce the critical pieces needed, sit next to the person and ask them about their families, how many kids do they have, what schools do the kids attend? Of all of the jobs that you have had, what was your favorite job? Of all of the jobs that you have had, which one paid the best, etc? There are ways to get information from individuals without reinforcing the idea their situation is their identity.

10. Stop manufactured gratitude.
Manufactured gratitude is the practice of inviting people in to audience the show of support/good will either publicly (the surprise gift or announcement to a perceived disadvantage person in front of a crowd of "stakeholders") or privately (sharing information of resolution with the expectation that the receiver of the information will be overjoyed/overcome with emotion) when you are literally doing what you are paid to do. This is a self-serving, dehumanizing practice that centers the giver's need for endorphins at the expense of the receiver's dignity. A recent experience with someone crystallized my understanding of how the centering of the giver is to the detriment of the receiver. Across the city of Indianapolis, students receive unsolicited gifts from donors with whom there is no relationship between the student, the family, or the donor. One student refused the shoes. She did not want them. She did not like them. The self-righteous outrage of the adults was palatable. "How can she not want these shoes?" one adult replied while surveying the shoes. Another chimed in, finger wagging the student saying: "You should be grateful to get new shoes." I cut into the conversation and told the young lady that she never has to be thankful for something that she did not ask for. It's a mantra that I live by sometimes—to the chagrin of my mother who was raised and still lives by the practice of southern gentility where one accepts and thanks the giver for things regardless of desirability. Even if you throw it away, you say thank you. I did not want to pass on the practice of dishonesty. I wanted the student and the adults around the student to know that it is always ok to refuse charity.
Christmastime, the unquestioned season of giving, is a time when this practice is on full display. Gift donations, toy and

food giveaways, and Christmas stores where families shop for toys, canned foods, jiffy cake mixes (with frosting!), gently used coats and shoes are celebrated during this season. Pictures of ingratiated families with volunteers, uber pious people of the cloth, and angelic servant leaders along with the bazillion of families served are presented across every spectrum of media. However, the other gifts that are given are not referenced. The gift of another reminder to the parent that they are poor. The gift of situating the giver in the position of power over the receiver. The gift of forced gratitude. The gift of continued distance between two humans that under different circumstances could actually be friends.
It is one of the worst forms of charity and should be examined from the purest lens of honesty—which will reveal that the practice is the combination of pimpin' and savior complex and should be abolished.

11. **Define the change and make the change.**
One of the hardest lessons that I have learned is that change in and of itself is not hard. Multiple changes are. Instability breeds fear, resistance, and apprehension. I recently relearned this lesson upon becoming an executive director of a mid-sized community organization. Four months into the role, I found myself asking: Why is this so hard? Infrastructure development, staff changes, funding cuts, internal were just a few of the things that were all happening at once. Team members were confused and afraid. There were too many changes happening at once. There was a lack of clarity of vision. Things were out of balance.
What did I do? I slowed down. I articulated with clarity the two prong vision: 1) to shift the multi-service center model to a community centered model; a joyful noise institution 2) to become an institution that can withstand shifts in philanthropy to ensure long term sustainability. After reiterating the vision across several communication channels, I began to execute behind the scene and forward facing changes. The first forward facing change happened during Thanksgiving. It was a simple yet important change. Balancing the knowledge that families needed food against the awful practice of forcing families to stand in lines to receive food vouchers only to struggle to find transportation

> to use them, I asked staff members to pick up vouchers (most literally identified food items for which the vouchers could be used), pick up the food, and deliver the food to our families. I abolished terminology that is not mission aligned. We do not do outreach. We do in reach. We reach into the community, commandeering the human capital that exists in the community to build community. Community service was redefined to center wholeness. Individuals entering the center for court ordered community service are reminded that they are part of our family. They are required to tell us how we can support them beyond signing off on the hours. The service that is assigned is to do things that bring them joy and return to the center to tell us about it. The team worked alongside me to expand and to reposition music programs across all ages, to the first floor of the building. Parent meetings were gamified with winners taking home cash prizes. I began describing the center as a A Joyful Noise Institution. The work is hard. Redesigning an infrastructure while redefining culture is hard. Loving the community is hard and will remain hard for many days to come. This is the cost of 100 years work.

The steps outlined are front of mind yet do not represent an exhaustive list. These are a few steps that can be taken as a measure to restore humanity to the experience of serving others. These are tactical steps that shift cultural norms and create a space for genuine connection. These steps should not require 100 years of board meetings, policy updates, and other administrative moves that often delay change making. The steps do however require strength, courage, and wisdom. The steps require the application of The Lords prayer in real time: Our father, who art in heaven, hallowed be thy name, thy kingdom come, thy will be done on earth as it is in heaven. Give us this day, our daily bread, forgive us our trespasses as we forgive those who trespass against us. Lead us not to temptation and deliver us from evil for Thine is the kingdom, and the power, and the glory forever. Amen. This work demands faith.

Faith

I first met Faith at a dinner organized by community members who dared to believe in the idea that communion and conversation could eventuate into systemic change.

The dinner was hosted by Indiana's Poet Laureate, Januarie. She introduced the post-dinner conversation by sharing her beautifully tragic story of overcoming. Her story was followed by others who shared their stories of overcoming, under employment, death, wrongful incarceration, physical and mental health issues, and unwarranted surveillance. There were doctors, professors, police, social workers, and other professionals in the room.

As the conversations around root causes unfolded, one word remained unspoken: RACISM. After forty minutes of unnecessary handwringing and half listening, I raised my voice and said "why are we not talking about racism? Racism is the root cause of all of this!" My emphatic proclamation was met with the obligatory head nods that signal silent discomfort. I grew frustrated with the nods, silence, and uneasy attempts to shift the heaviness of the statement and left.

A few weeks later I ran into Faith outside of Broadway UMC. After talking with her, she invited Mike Mather and me to tour one of the clinics for which she is responsible.

The clinic is in predominately Black and brown "low income" community. Unlike other clinics that I have been in, this clinic was clean and the staff reflected the demographic of the community. It is a great service delivery system, that even has community health advocates that visit families in their homes! The accommodations also include transportation vouchers and connections to "additional resources." The clinic goes to great lengths to support families yet the number of patients that return for follow up appointments is subpar.

Throughout the course of the tour, staff members across the hierarchy talked about the work and the people served. The language used to describe the residents as "city's most vulnerable" indicated a lack of institutional analysis.

When discussing the challenge of getting residents to attend follow up visits, the superlative adjective, "most vulnerable" keep ringing in my ears.

This language inherently assumed deficiency in patients. This language further reinforced the power inequities that allow doctors to blame patients for health problems as opposed to examining systemic causes of ailments plaguing black and brown communities. This language is the antithesis of abundance and joy; the very subjects that brought Faith and I together.

Faith is unapologetically white. She does not apologize for her whiteness. She does not pretend to be anything other than who she is; a white woman with power in an institution that affects the lives of people every day. Though not apologetic about her whiteness, Faith is on a journey to understand how racism has shaped and informed the way in which we live in this country. To her credit, it did not take witnessing the murder of a black man on national television for her to realize that racism and the power of whiteness affords her particular advantages that are unavailable to non-white people.

Faith has two superpowers. One superpower is in her willingness to publicly admit that which she does not know. I attended a public meeting focused on the development of "health zones" across targeted zip codes. The goal of the zones is to improve health outcomes. Faith was one of the experts speaking about the social determinants of health and the structures that were being built to address disparities. During the question and answer section, I approached and asked what changes are happening within the training of the medical teams to address the disparities? Specifically, how does this work address the racism endemic to the health care system that drives the disparities? Faith's response was honest: "I don't know. I don't know that it does but this is a start." The vulnerability of her response was on full display to everyone in the room. She could have given a shallow yet palatable political response. She opted for honesty.

Faith's second superpower is her willingness to use the privileges of whiteness and power to effect immediate impact within her institution and in the community at large. As a member of the team responsible for the construction and opening of a new health center, Faith fought for and won the battle to commission artists from the community who would have the PAID opportunity to design the art that now decorates the multistory building.

Recognizing and using personal power is critical. Institutions are not moved by those who operate from a place of subservience nor are they moved from a place of timidity. In order to do what will be described below you have to have the intestinal fortitude to recognize where you have power and how to use it.

Abundance+Joy=Risk-taking

At this point one may wonder what does the story of Faith have to do with 100 years work? The answer—in my mind—goes back to epigenetics. When a person or group of people has lived in a space of suppression, oppression, and survival, the DNA mutates and joy and abundance receptors are interrupted.

It can take generations to cultivate the courage needed to risk seeing and experiencing joy and abundance. Many Christians will understand the story of Ezekiel in the land of dry bones. Faith's journey toward understanding the Abundance+Joy=Risk equation eventuated in the creation of staff abundance circle opportunities.

Faith hired me and De'Amon to walk clinical staff through a process of self-discovery. The question that I, as the leader of the circles, sought to answer was: how do individual experiences of joy and abundance in the workplace affect patient outcomes? The answer is captured in the following story:

One participant in a conversation stated that prior to engaging with the circle, she received mediocre patient evaluations. She received positive feedback on medical knowledge yet damning feedback on questions regarding her knowledge of the patient.

She was initially frustrated by what appeared to be contradictory statements. After attending a few circles, she understood what the patients were messaging. She didn't know them. She didn't know anything about them as *humans*; she only knew them as their illness.

Fast forward to the last session (each cohort participated in 4 sessions) and she was ecstatic to report that she was consistently receiving great patient evaluations. Patient feedback included feelings of being seen and known! How did she do this? She changed the sequence and content of the questions that she was asking. She reported that she began asking patients the same questions that were asked in the circle: Who loves you? How would your friends describe you? When was the last time you danced? What's your favorite color?

She added patient responses to their medical chart and each time a patient returned, she would start the visit with a question related to the answers provided or she would notice if they were wearing their favorite color and sometimes she would even pretend to dance as she conducted the check up.

Seek and Ye Shall Find

Another participant was initially reluctant to engage in conversation. She entered the work with the preconceived idea that the work was centered around racism. Though racism was a part of the experience, the larger part focused on where abundance lived in her life. Throughout the course of time together, she disclosed that she had a very difficult life and never felt love. The only response that I could muster to that statement was, Who or what do you love? After a twenty-second pause (which felt like forever), she responded she loves playing in the bell choir at her church.

This conversation took place months after pandemic restrictions were being lifted. As she talked about playing the bells she jubilantly shared that she and her friend were going on a cruise where they would play bells for Sandi Patty! After sharing the details of the planned trip, she shared it never occurred to her to ask her patients or teammates who or what do they love and why.

She committed to asking the questions. A year later, I randomly decided to attend a church that I visit infrequently. Upon arrival, who do I see? This same person who not only played bells that day but served me communion as well. A joyful spirit is contagious. This woman had to strain her eyes, heart, and spirit to find and experience a love that she believed that she was lacking. I believe that she is a better practitioner and that her teammates and patients are better for it.

The work with the staff had positive health outcomes. The outcomes are measurable and impactful. Did it cure diabetes? No. I am willing to risk saying that it cured blindness.

These are just two of the many transformational stories of how focused work on abundance and joy affected the culture and delivery of service to patients in the community health centers. There are a few tangible things to note related to the work.

The work is risky. Faith made the case for the work to her bosses without a lot of information about how it would look and without any predetermined evidence that it would have any impact. Faith made an offer to the staff using only her personal belief in the power of abundance and joy.

Informed relationships matter. Though Faith was willing to take a risk, she did not do so blindly. She and I each other another as humans who know what we are doing and what we are talking about. This is important to note as increasingly more organizations use the term "relationship" without clearly defining what it means.

The work contradicts itself all of the time. The contradictions are natural and to be expected because humans are involved. This work was simultaneously relational and transactional. Over the course of the work, relationships were formed. And at the end of the four sessions, the relationships ended. This does not mitigate the impact or importance but is a fact that is too often glossed over.

The greatest risks in this work are the removal of blinders and the willingness to *see* all of the abundance and joy that exists in every circumstance. This is risky because once a person or group of people experiences the life-changing power of joy and abundance, they begin to imagine a world where others have the experience. The desire to share the experience releases a courage that propels one to challenge long-standing belief systems and power structures.

100 years is more than a lifetime for many people. 100 years is not a requirement. Faith is a white woman born in and from Texas. Texas, the reason why we celebrate Juneteenth. Texas where there is an additional tax added to the sale of a belt buckle based on the size of the buckle! It did not take Faith 100 years to act. It took less than one. It may have taken many breaths, conversations with bosses, and other efforts but it did *not* take 100 years. Or maybe Faith is the manifestation of the 100 years that it takes to reshape a gene pool?

"For the master's tools will never dismantle the master's house."[2] In order to provide an acceptable exegesis on this statement, I would have to write a separate book—and I would fail. The power of word and imagery represented in this statement belongs to my ancestor. In fairness to myself and in honor of my ancestor, I suggest that those who are reading this purchase and read anything written by Audre Lorde; specifically, *Sister Outsider*.

The application of the statement in relationship to 100 years work requires an examination of the master's tools and how they are employed to maintain subjugation and suppression. This is not an exhaustive inventory of the tools. It is an analysis of a few tools that currently dominate work across communities.

Master's Tool #1: Illusion of Power Sharing

The illusory sharing of power is a tool used to convince unheard populations that sitting at the master's table, advising the master, and serving as a thought partner with the master *is* real power. The seat at the table paradigm is powerful because of the seductive promise of being heard. Unheard communities have been convinced by the master that a seat at the table will eventuate in change. Periodically, unheard communities have challenged this idea by demanding to control the table (bring my own table) and seat availability. The problem with each approach is that the language used to describe the approach to power and the exercise of power are directly drawn from the master's tool box. It is painful to witness communities come to the understanding that sitting at any table is a passive existence and designed to give dominant populations an opportunity to give ear to what is happening in communities without ever having to *hear* the voices.

Human history is the greatest teacher on the irrational belief in power sharing. The history of colonization and the subsequent wars for freedom is a clear example of this.

Reversing the impact of this practice not only requires courage, it requires a Machiavellian understanding of how the powerful can respond.

Throughout my work with a white led–female run organization, I met a woman who had the courage to do something that I have yet to see mirrored across other organizations. After the murder of George Floyd, she and I engaged in a conversation about power. She wanted to make a real difference in the organization's approach to race in Indianapolis.

Her role in the organization controlled access to expensive professional development and training opportunities. The makeup of her committee was racially diverse. The committee however lacked class, political, and sexuality diversity. As we talked about what change would look like from her perspective, she concluded that she did not want to open up more seats at the table. She wanted the existing seats at the table to be occupied by different people. In her mind, and I agreed, adding more seats does not shift power. Her next step was amazing: she invited four of the seven members of her committee to rotate off. She did not offer a preamble except to say that she wanted to move the committee in a different direction.

In true Machiavellian form, the detractors' response was quick and brutal. The response was loud, harsh, racist, classist, and slanderous. The woman was accused of "performing racial justice," desiring to bring down the organization, and "forgetting how she got the position in the first place."

She was also accused of using her power and privilege to bully other members in the organization. The woman endured attacks from within and outside of the organization. Throughout the relentless attacks, she did not waver. She remains with the organization.

The majority of the committee is made up of those who were intentionally pushed to the margins. The majority of the committee members are people of diverse backgrounds. This majority now controls access to the opportunities that were once denied them. There is no power sharing. There are no extra seats at the table.

Master's Tool #2: Moralizing

As a sociology student at DePauw University, we played a power simulation game. The idea of the game was to demonstrate power inequities by challenging each participant to amass enough power (represented in colored dots) to ascend to the ruling class. The trick was that the distribution of the dots needed was concentrated to one group with only a few dots available to the rest of the class. Students outside of the group where the power was concentrated were instructed to use the power of persuasion, bartering, and other means to convince those with power to share the power.

As students engaged in the activity, I knocked the green (power) dots out of the hand of one student. I offered to help pick them up but only returned a portion of the dots. In another instance, I gently took dots from a student as the student poured a glass of punch. Throughout the fifteen-minute exercise, I was able to amass enough dots to become a part of the ruling class.

When the class gathered back together, we were told to sit with the group to which they belonged based on the number and color of dots. I sat with the ruling class. The persons from whom I stole dots were aghast as were the other members of the ruling class. Those from whom I had stolen were no longer in the ruling class. Those who were in the ruling class found that the attempt to self-segregate and lock others out of the group had failed. One student was so perplexed that he yelled, "How did you get in this group?" He further demanded to count my dots (which I refused to allow).

The professor, holding back laughter, asked me how I managed to ascend to the group given the limited number of dots and the way that they were distributed. I told the class that I stole the number of dots needed to be a part of the ruling class.

The moral judgment that followed the admission was something to behold. The class, even those who were not a part of the ruling class, could not believe that I would steal. The litany of moral judgments went on until the professor interrupted and posed the basic question: Is it fair to expect those who are oppressed by the rules to obey the rules?

Moralizing the behavior of groups for whom the rules do not work is a powerful tool of the Master. This tactic shifts the conversation from systemic oppression to individual responsibility without questioning the beneficiaries of unjust rules.

This practice takes the stage each time the unheard raise voices and arms against the apparatuses of oppression. This was and remains evident each time groups rally together against police brutality. While the protests against racialized terror periodically grab national attention, it is the daily moralizing of behavior that is concerning.

Consider the amount of information required of individuals who are poor to prove poverty in order to receive minimal assistance. Consider the amount of energy expended to prevent welfare, unemployment, and child care subsidy fraud. The moralizing of behavior is a way to exempt majority institutions and beneficiaries from examining the structural barriers that incentivizes the "breaking of the rules" as the rules cannot apply if they prohibit living an abundant life.

Master's Tool #3: Compromise

In the late 1980s, I attended a conference in Minnesota. During the conference there were many debates about the state of education, the work of teachers, and the role of unions. At some point, a well-meaning attendee stated, "everyone just needs to figure out a way to compromise on the issues" to which a self-identified Native American responded, "we tried compromise and you see where that got us."

I applauded the statement. Compromise is code for status quo maintenance. Compromise does not shift power in any significant ways. It does, however, rob the room of imagination and the potential for transformation.

Master's Tool #4: Responsive Narrative

Responsive narratives are a direct response to the denigrating stereotypes that have been/continue to be created about non-white people in this country. Generations of formerly enslaved Black people adopted narratives of exceptionalism and respectability politics to address the negative narrative. Immigrant communities adopted and continue to maintain the narrative of meritocracy. The gross power of this tool is the ability for the master to manipulate the spirit of oppressed groups to the point that energy is expended attempting to prove the master wrong. Another gross component of this tool is that by focusing on proving the master wrong, a space for the master's participation in the narrative is inadvertently created. A recent example of this is the growing number of Black Joy celebrations taking place across the country.

I am a proponent of celebrating Black Joy every day! The problem with the public display of Black Joy, at least in Indianapolis, is that it is done for the consumption of white people.

The Black Joy celebration from inception was designed in response to media representations of Black and Brown people in the news. A primary goal of the celebration is to show white people that Black and Brown people in the city engage in activities that do not include "crime."

The premise reeks of internalized racism. The idea that we have to prove that we are multidimensional humans is harmful to the collective psyche. Importantly, responding to the media's representation of our community by hosting a Black Joy event assumes that Black joy is an event; not something that is experienced *every single day* on porches, in kitchens, on playgrounds, in churches, and so on.

In addition to harming the communal psyche, Black Joy and other events that are hosted as a way of dispelling the master's narrative buy into the ideas that teaching and/or earning the master's anything is something to which the community should aspire.

Finally, this craftiness of this tool cannot be understated because inevitably, the master is invited to the table to have a voice at the table; to be a full-on participant in the narrative that would not exist if the master viewed and treated all as human.

Master's Tool #5: Weaponized Philanthropy

Conditional philanthropy is weaponized philanthropy. When I was younger, a member of my church endowed a scholarship on the condition that no black person could ever serve as the chair person. The use of money to enforce antiquated racial norms represents weaponized philanthropy. Forced prayers, denunciation of "life styles", exclusion of non-married families fetc are all forms of this toxic practice. Churches, schools, and social service entities perpetuate this behavior. One of the more glaring ways that this practice is demonstrated is the "prove it" method. This is the method that requires individuals to "prove" that they are worthy of support by documenting trauma, poverty, etc in order to access support while simultaneously demonstrating how they will self sustain upon receiving the support. This method serves the dual purpose of fulfilling the goals/objectives of the service model while blaming the individual for their circumstance. Most often, after demonstrating "worth", individuals receive services which is counter intutitive because across multiple studies it has been proven that in most cases, the real solution is money; individual agency and choice. This fact was proven on a national scale during the pandemic when families received cash subsidies. According to the Center on Budget and Policy Priorities, the first two rounds of the stimulus lifted 11.7 million people above the poverty line. If this can happen within two years, imagine the impact of 100 years worth economic stimulus going to families that the organization is designed to "help!"

The weaponization of philanthropy centers on the philanthropic community's insistence on seeing and treating humans as widgets in need of fixing. A google search of grant requirements for many philanthropic organizations reveals the creation of applicant-funder codependence rooted in deficiency which in turns requires organizations to diagnose and treat the community as less than. The co-dependence maintains the power dynamics that prohibit imagination, innovation, joy and love.

There is however a growing movement within the philanthropic community to shift this power imbalance; I call it philanthropic disarmament.

The trust based philanthropic movement is working to reimagine philanthropy. Trust based philanthropy recognizes that relationships are the economies that effect real change. This form of philanthropy engages with all that the money touches (staff members, residents, power brokers, etc) with the goal of creating and maintaining long term relationships. It further interrogates narratives to discern areas where love and honesty are dominant and invests in those areas. It is the closest thing to investing in Joy that I have witnessed to date.

Master's Tool #6: Public Image

After the public executions of black people across the country, the masters took to the airwaves and to social media to express their commitment to the groups that they systemically oppressed on a daily basis. In response to the murder of George Floyd, Nike released the "don't do it" campaign while paying less than livable wages to store associates across the country.

Public promises in wake of national tragedies are used to manipulate emotions and to create a false perception. The promises are often unexamined and the public rallies behind messaging while failing to interrogate the companies' behavior.

Extrapolating the common denominators that exist between public image and actual practice can take 100 years. It is important to note however that without examining behavior, the master's tool will always, always be used to maintain the house; never to destroy it.

The master's toolbox is ever changing. It is for this reason that we must push ourselves to engage in the Socratic method of self-interrogation. The practice of self-reflection when engaging in this work cannot be overstated. The tools are operative in every part of the culture. It is incumbent upon those who engage in this work to begin the practice by asking difficult questions like:

What measuring tools am I using to determine impact (is it more love, more joy, more laughter?)

Who am I talking to that will push me to, shake loose this skin, so that I can live into this work in ways imagined and unimagined?

What new life am I encouraging/co-creating?

CHAPTER 4

Building from What We Have

De'Amon Harges

The Green Book

There are principles in an abundant community that cultivate opportunities for people to fall in love with one another.

Gifts must be looked for in order to be seen.

Gifts must be unwrapped. Find ways to get people to use their gifts with others.

Celebrate people's gifts in the public square.

We are what we need, if we take the time to listen deeply to people's stories and find ways to connect them to the other stories around us. One night at dinner with Mike Mather and John McKnight, after an event in Cincinnati, John talked about some of his regrets. He especially mentioned formalizing some of the work of the ABCD Institute. He worried it would take away from actual community practices.

One of those practices was the creation of the asset map. John talked about people making an asset map, putting the information in databases, and letting it sit unused. In my experience, a file cabinet of people's gifts, talents, dreams, and passions is fairly useless. John's late-night comments got me thinking about making certain we put these stories in people's hearts, not only in a file cabinet. It nudged us to find ways to connect those gifts and bring mutual delight.

Jody Kretzmann and John McKnight wrote a book called *Building Communities from the Inside Out: A Path Toward Finding and Mobilizing a Community's Assets.* People often refer to it as "the Green Book."

The book is about finding pathways to discover a community's assets and mobilize them. It was written before I knew anything about asset-based community development. At least, that's what I thought.

I came to understand that the lessons John and Jody talk about in the Green Book, I already knew, because they were the way of my people: my grandpa, my parents, and their neighbors. I knew it by its stories, not by what it was formally called.

When I was growing up, I used to hear stories about how people found their way to where they were going. My grandfather and grandmother would tell stories about escaping southern brutality. Telling stories was a way of survival.

This practice, common among my people, moved from house to house and city to city. Wherever I landed, there were folk, people who looked like me, telling the same journey.

This got me thinking about how my family got to South Bend, and how Black people got north.

I came across an African American travel guide created in the mid-1930s. It was designed to keep African American and Jewish families safe as they traveled in the Jim Crow era.

The creator was Victor Hugo Green, an African American postal worker who was interested in people's stories. He started out paying people a dollar for each encounter they would share. This travel guide was called the Green Book.

This Green Book was an actual asset map. It not only connected people, it saved lives. It found ways to connect them, and often it carried stories of entrepreneurship, arts, culture, and love. This Green Book became the foundation and the evidence of how Black Wall Street, in Tulsa, was built. As the old saying goes, "People only learn what they already know."

The Green Book was not something put into a file cabinet. It lived in a world of abundance. It took the knowledge people gathered and shared it. It became testimony to an abundant world even in the midst of scarcity. It reminds us that the main ingredient of community is love.

A lesson from a learning journey I took to Washington, DC, helped me see our next steps.

Vision is the destroyer of essence.

Vision is being a witness, not a creator.

Failure is an option, even a necessity.

Who are the archetypes of a beloved community?

In the summer of 2002, my wife Janeen and I were expecting our daughter, DeJanea. I was a first-grade teacher on the west side of Chicago, getting ready to go on paternity leave.

I got a call from Mike Mather, who was still at Broadway Christian Parish in South Bend, Indiana, and from Lyle West, a member there, inviting me on a learning journey to Washington, DC, to visit the Adams Morgan neighborhood. Mike wanted us to see some of its community development projects and meet people doing interesting work.

On the first night, we visited the Potter's House, a coffee shop and third space. It was a bustling social bank where people exchanged imagination and social capital.

That afternoon, their speaker was Gordon Cosby, a pastor at the center of what was happening in that neighborhood. The room was filled with young church planters from the Vineyard movement in the UK.

Gordon was there to inspire young, faithful leaders to serve God outside the walls of the church. As he told the stories of his work, he said something that shocked the room. In his gruff southern drawl, he said, "Vision is the destroyer of essence."

I was baffled, because I thought having a vision was a good thing. It took me months to wrestle with what Gordon had said. Back in my neighborhood, I started to realize that people had a vision for us, for our beautiful community, despite its low wealth, low income, and plentiful police runs.

We were defined only in the language of scarcity. The northwest area held 40 percent of all the city's vacancies. It was seen as blighted. Many organizations brought in programs to fix what they saw. They used words like "make this a better place," "this place needs to be revitalized," and "we must create the tax base."

No one was coming in trying to hurt anyone, but it hurt. The essence of our place was beauty. It was love and abundance, alongside the harder things people named. Those well-meaning commentators from outside our community had vision, but they could not see the essence. They could not see the beauty of entrepreneurs like Dominic Moses, or environmentalists like Tysha Ahmed, who lives on 31st and Clifton, or people like Mr. William Ryder, an imaginator whose art celebrated people young and old.

The do-gooders named only what they could see. Their vision would have destroyed the essence. Wildstyle, a young man with a sharp eye and a wicked sense of the truth, was one of the first neighbors to learn what those casting "vision" were up to. They told me a story about potentially hundreds of thousands of dollars going into our neighborhood to beautify it.

Wildstyle took the list of artists we had discovered in our neighborhood and, along with two other neighbors, shared it with the group. He said, "You will not beautify our neighborhood with artists from outside it. We have plenty here. We will help you use the artists we already have to share the stories of beauty."

They were excited about the idea and asked Wildstyle for the list of artists. He resisted handing it over. He proposed instead that they give the money to The Learning Tree, to be invested in the hands of the artists already there.

Wildstyle and a few neighbors would help facilitate this. He talked with them about hiring young videographers and storytellers to witness the abundance on display, because often people wouldn't believe us.

It's one of the reasons the "visioners" from outside wanted the list. Wildstyle wanted to make sure it stayed in the hands of people in the neighborhood. The last thing he proposed was that we invest in people we call healers, the ones who always celebrated what people were doing, and have them throw gatherings we called "salons."

The artists told their stories on doors found discarded in alleys, left over from renovation projects in the neighborhood.

We called the exhibition of the artists' pieces "Perception: What's Behind the Door." It illustrated the gifts, talents, and dreams of around 52 artists in our neighborhood.

Folks from all backgrounds participated: individuals, families, artists, poets, and entrepreneurs. We had no idea this many people needed to be seen the way they wanted to be seen. We paid each participant a stipend and ended up with 150 doors.

The problem with abundance is that you can have too much of a good thing. We had no place to store the doors, so they ended up on the porches of each participant for about three or four blocks. It was a door takeover.

I got a call from a local news station asking about the doors. I asked, "Why is it so important to do a story about these doors?" The reporter replied, "Well, I was here for a police run, and I was starting to think that was all this place is about. As I noticed the doors, I became more curious about this community." Cosby's line, "Vision is the destroyer of essence," came back to me. We were finding ways to illustrate the essence.

One day, Wildstyle confessed that my excitement hadn't lessened his doubt. He had seen many people come to his community and communities like ours. He said it wasn't until he followed me around that the invisible became visible. He would bring his camera and snap photos. He shared them online: the doors on empty houses, blown-up photos of fathers with their children, mothers teaching art classes, and more. They were larger than life. Something shifted as residents started to see themselves as contributors, even though it had always been true.

They were being celebrated by storytellers. We learned that in a beloved community, joy is precipitated by being seen, and it takes storytellers like Wildstyle, who are abundant in such neighborhoods, for gifts to be seen and used.

This changed not only how we saw ourselves, but how others saw us. It increased the number of people who wanted to invest in us and collaborate with us, not because we were different, but because we had gifts to share.

Our neighbors have agency and power. We knew it in governing ourselves, in running our own company, in setting the agenda for our own neighborhood, and in making the world aware of the gifts we have to give.

Outside organizations readjusted their eyes to see our neighbors as full of vitality, needing to be unveiled rather than revitalized. We didn't need resuscitation, we needed celebration, as we began to recognize our power. We started using our own landscape as a gathering place. One thing I learned in my old neighborhood is that the way to get people to share power is to get them to parties, outside of institutions like the church. Institutional life is formal. At Broadway, when I was the Roving Listener, I would have people from the development corporation and from the church come to meet the neighbors from the block I had spent time on that week.

I wanted the development corporation people and the church people to see what I had uncovered. We held these meetings in neighbors' homes. We never held them at the church, because there the church was perceived as having more power than the residents.

When representatives from the institutions entered a home, they were given one instruction: "You are here to listen." The only time they were allowed to speak was to ask a discerning question. The goal was to invite people to fall in love with one another. This is acting out of, and creating, the epigenetics of joy.

Chapter 4

Asking New Questions to Find the Next Generation of Joy Finders

Just like where I grew up in South Bend, Indiana, our neighborhood in Indianapolis was full of people related to one another. My aunt Marilyn and her children lived across the street from us. Other cousins lived a couple of blocks away.

When I moved to Indianapolis, I discovered the same thing. The rumor was that ours was a transitional neighborhood, that people were moving through and weren't rooted there. That isn't true.

Like South Bend, the Mapleton Fall Creek and Near Northwest neighborhoods held deep, interconnected roots, deep as the roots of baobab trees.

Some of the notable families in Mapleton Fall Creek were the Sharps, the Buddhas, and the Evans. In my new neighborhood, the Highbaughs, the Boyds, and the McIlwaines were families solving problems and causing problems. They governed the community: its relationships, its justice, and its economics.

In the Mapleton Fall Creek neighborhood, the Evans family was the second largest, behind the Buddhas. I met Trienna Evans through her oldest son, Sean.

I played pickup football with him, his cousins, and other young men and women in the community. Sean, like most teens I know, was giving his mother a hard time.

Sean is a gifted athlete, and also gifted at reading people. He paid attention, and he was a leader among his friends. He was charismatic and headstrong.

Sean would get in trouble at school and was often suspended, so I got to see him a little more than I should have. As I got to know him, I asked him to introduce me to his parents. Sean was the oldest of seven. I learned he got his smile from his mother.

That's when I met Trienna. I walked the four blocks to her home, and Sean introduced me to his mother and the rest of the family. I had my daughter, DeJanea, with me in a backpack carrier. Everyone looked skeptical when I walked in, a reaction to my dreadlocks and my painted Amtrak overalls. (I am an artist, after all.) I didn't know it at the time, but they thought I was homeless and needed a place to stay.

We all come from somewhere. We have a history that tells us who we are and what gifts we have to share.

When I talked with Trienna about Sean and met the rest of his siblings, I knew she was a good mother. She was gifted at doing a lot with very little. She is the kind of person who smiles and looks up even when things are hard.

I got to know Trienna better later. Though she worked in food service, her true gifts were hospitality, listening, and caring for others. Trienna is a healer.

Jalen and Jada Evans

The Evans twins were the youngest of Trienna's children: Jada and Jalen. Jada is older by a few minutes. She likes to claim Jalen, a soft-spoken young man with a quiet confidence, as if he were the big brother.

Jada is always poised, with an outgoing smile like her mother, solid as an oak. She doesn't mince words. She finds beauty in simple things.

She loves football and basketball, and she is now a young mother. She was not even 30 when I left the Roving Listener role at Broadway.

Young people started to multiply the Roving Listener work in new ways. Jada and Jalen were children when their siblings began doing it in the summer.

The church had been running a traditional summer program. It was called JSP, the Jubilee Summer Program.

The Jubilee Summer Program began after the church expanded its summer offerings beyond basketball for the boys and cheerleading for the girls. They built a more well-rounded program, intended to be taught by parents from the community. The only problem was that it still ran in the framework, spirit, and power Broadway had created. It was not a bad thing. It simply wasn't changing things for the better.

Now change was coming again. Mike pushed those of us in the church to imagine something different. So we hired young people to begin doing what I had been doing. We paid them to meet their neighbors, to find their neighbors' gifts, talents, dreams, and passions, and to connect them with other people who cared about the same things.

We called it "Name, Bless, and Connect." As it grew, it became more and more intergenerational.

As I mentioned, decades ago I heard Gordon Cosby, the founder of Church of the Saviour in Washington, DC, say that "vision is the destroyer of essence." What a complex statement that is. And if it's true, our visionaries can be destroyers.

In hindsight, I see what Broadway was attempting in this new, evolved way: changing from holding the vision to sitting as a witness to the essence of the work around us. When we hired young people to go listen to their neighbors, it decentralized who had the power to listen.

Our first group included Jada's brother Brandon, along with Charita, Kyla, and Adam, brothers and sisters from around the block. Two adult neighbors, Teri and Martha, led it. This was different for them too.

Trienna would spend time with the Roving Youth Corps at Broadway. When people saw her walking down the street, it opened doors for the young people that had been closed to them before.

Trienna's oldest son was one of the original Roving Youth Corps. When Trienna came along, her younger children would tag along. This is how I met Jada and Jalen. Jada likes to tell me, "I was only a baby when I met you."

I was born to do this work. The Roving Listener role was created and named for what I naturally do out in the world. The church didn't start with a job description. They simply asked whether I was interested in getting paid for what I was already doing in the neighborhood.

They built on what I had to contribute. They started with the gifts in their hands, or in this case, in mine.

Moving from the power of vision to the power of witnessing what is already going on was hard. But the young people would walk through the neighborhood every week, and they would listen. Montell O'Bannon's story was especially striking.

Ms. O'Bannon, a wise elder in our neighborhood, was raising her grandchildren. Montell visited an older gentleman and his wife who told him they had been married for 46 years. Montell, only 10 or 11 at the time, came back from the walk amazed. He said "46 years" with emphasis, like it was a miracle.

It was powerful to see a young man notice something other young people didn't, something we would have assumed he didn't care about.

Montell would visit his neighbors three days a week and spend two days that summer in a room we called "the fishes and loaves room."

This is where the multiplication happened. Young people put up brightly colored Post-it notes, each with a person's name, one of their gifts, and the block they lived on. They grouped the notes by common interests.

Once they had three or more in a group, they would throw a dinner. This went on for about two summers. The listeners grew from 7 to 15, with a few stragglers along the way. Younger siblings and friends joined in. Jada and Jalen were less than 10 years old, but they came because their older siblings, cousins, and neighbors were Roving Listeners.

This was the listeners' job. They were getting paid for it. It became a kind of competition. They created their own lingo. "We're roving today." It became part of who they were.

This was great. Then, the second summer, more young people wanted in. I was learning my own lessons about connecting. My role as the Roving Listener was officially coming to an end. I didn't know that the end only meant my job description would evolve. My work was changing, and so was I. I was asked to spend more time outside the neighborhood, telling people about the remarkable people inside it.

I had to split my time and spend a couple of days a week outside the neighborhood. I chose the Chatterbox Bar in downtown Indianapolis, because I heard it was a happening place.

I could get cocktails and listen to music, but my job was to tell three stories to people in the bar about people in our neighborhood, then gather three stories from people in the bar to bring back to my neighbors, then find ways to connect them in person so they could see each other.

One of those visits connected me with Jeremy Efroymson. Jeremy is about my age, a young innovator from a philanthropic family. He was one of the members stewarding the family foundation. They gave mostly to creative endeavors.

After a couple of drinks, Jeremy said there was a shift going on in how they thought about their philanthropy. He asked me about the gardeners in our neighborhood.

I told him about Mrs. Kimbrough, who had created a talking cookbook, and Mrs. Jackson, who grew beans on her front porch, not only for food but for shade.

The philanthropist seemed excited, so I invited him to visit and meet some of the gardeners.

I organized a gathering with Miss Rose, who lives a block and a half from the church. The day came. Around noon, the philanthropist showed up at the church. I met him on the front steps on the 29th Street side, stopped him, explained he was at the wrong place, and walked him a block down to Miss Rose's house.

The gardeners were waiting for him, chatty and happy for the visit. They didn't know anything about him yet, except that he was a guest who wanted to meet them. I left him there and went back to the church to finish some work.

About two hours later, the philanthropist showed up and said he wanted to write a check. He wrote it for an initial 25 thousand dollars to Broadway, for our gardening program.

WE DIDN'T HAVE A GARDENING PROGRAM!

We had gardeners who gardened!

I knew that when Jeremy came back to the church, he would be schooled in Black wisdom and artistry in action. I didn't know how much schooling he had gotten until he returned.

The gardeners took the money and built a hoop house. The church had little to nothing to do with it, intentionally, except for the meals with the gardeners, which other residents hosted.

The gardeners helped one another dream and discover new possibilities for their craft, and this inspired Miss Rose and her neighbors to come up with more ideas.

They were already doing this in their neighborhood. This gave them the chance to expand it and share tools, seeds, and practices with one another. I also learned a big lesson about economics: stories are currency. Sharing stories isn't only for mutual entertainment. It is a way to watch people's worlds expand.

You probably think I'm talking about those low-income gardeners. No, I'm talking about Jeremy Efroymson. He got to learn what was available and possible in our neighborhood, instead of his statistics about scarcity and need.

He came to realize that every gardener in our community was needed, and he wanted to invest in them.

This practice taught me to call myself a social banker. I started finding ways to share my neighborhood's stories with the broader world. It was a way to take the testimony time at church and amplify it.

By 2007, it was becoming harder to live in Mapleton Fall Creek. This was during the 2007-2008 housing crisis that left a lot of Black and brown people under bad loans. I looked at about 75 homes in that community and couldn't settle on one. I finally picked a beautiful home in a neighborhood adjacent to my former hood.

It was called United Northwest. My cross streets were Clifton and 33rd. I continued to help out around Broadway, but the young people took over the reins by 2011.

Jalen was running the Roving Youth summer program, and a year later his sister, Jada, joined him. They became a dynamic duo. They modernized the work so young people could do the same listening and connecting, but in their own way.

Jalen did this during the summers while going to school in Vincennes, a college in southern Indiana. Jada, by now a teen mom, finished her schooling and decided to focus on the healing arts: listening, connecting, and caring for people. She was a natural. She was also good with the other young people.

She had come a long way from the outgoing four-year-old I first met with her siblings. As the program went on, Jada and Jalen would call me for advice.

They did the program right, the budgeting right, even the grant writing right. They were in charge, and the practice was in even better hands than mine.

Back in 2008, even with the financial crisis, there was hope in our neighborhood as the country welcomed its first Black president. Earlier that year, I found myself in the motherland, in South Africa. It was surreal. It was post-apartheid.

I was in a township of Cape Town called Gugulethu. Rev. Mather had invited me to be the Roving Listener for a month at a Presbyterian church named J. L. Zwane. They were famous for their work supporting community members with HIV and AIDS.

I am shy by nature, curious, positive, and creative, and I love watching people be celebrated. This served me well in South Africa. It was walking through a completely new door, and I loved it. The people were warm and kind. In Gugulethu, people had even less than the people in my neighborhood. In the month I was there, I learned a lot, including how people greet each other. They say, "Sawubona," which means "I see you." This was something my neighbors needed to hear and know, that we are seen.

In Gugulethu, they struggled with the same things we did. They weren't seen as gifted. I worked with the people I met, the people at the church, and the people at the Truth and Reconciliation Commission to hire cooks and photographers from Gugulethu to reveal the many gifts around them.

100-year work requires a deep listening that learns people's stories in ways social service organizations, philanthropies, and religious organizations have not.

No wonder the results are so poor. They don't really know the tools, the people, they are working with.

Resisting Scarcity

At the beginning of this journey, it was so important that my friend Mike had the foresight to resist scarcity practices. We had a partnership with the local community development corporation in our neighborhood.

100-year work requires developing new practices, which may run counter, very counter, to the old ones.

It's not so hard to do the new thing. What is hard is stepping away from the old thing, so the new thing has space to take root and grow.

Mike knew that while the development corporation said they would support this plan, with me as the Roving Listener, they didn't really understand it. Mike also saw the genius in my disruption. He wasn't a great supervisor to me, but he was a great cheerleader.

It was powerful to discover myself in an official role built on my natural practice. I learned that I had an incredible eye for what brought people joy.

The beauty of what we did in the Mapleton Fall Creek neighborhood and at the church where I worked was that we cultivated a social infrastructure for an abundant ecosystem. It also gave me room to make space for the agency of others in our neighborhood.

This is where I started to understand that the greatest need in anyone is the need to be needed. I hired Akua, my friend Yusuf's daughter, to record and transcribe the conversations.

My church gave a platform to people's gifts for exchange in the wider community. I was able to flourish and master my gift because of Mike's willingness to let go of his "white man power" and let me flourish.

Otherwise, I would have been buried in needs surveys that only reinforced the idea of neighbors as a needy people rather than a needed people. We would have missed the potential that was there.

Years after I started this work, after we began paying young people in the summer to listen for the gifts the way I had, listening programs started popping up all over: one in Richmond, Virginia, one in Macon, Georgia, one in Houston, Texas, one in Wichita, Kansas.

I was being asked to scale this idea and practice. Mike would often step in and tell people we can't scale this.

Mike would say, "You don't have a De'Amon." The point was to look for the people and the gifts already present where you serve, live, and play. The point was to change the questions from needs-based to potential-based, questions about what's present, not what's absent.

The point was to celebrate what we all bring together. The point was not to hoard the giving to ourselves, but to change the odds for everyone by using our social capital.

I call myself the Original Roving Listener because of how the idea developed. As I mentioned, I'm the first one to do this work, and that is because of the practices of my grandparents.

My grandfather was a John 10:10 person. He would quote the verse at community gatherings before people left. He loved where Jesus says, "I have come so that you might have life abundantly." They believed this.

Over the years, I have developed a few practices. Here are the ones I live by:

We have what we need and who we need. Because South Bend, Indiana, was so segregated in the 40s, 50s, and 60s, my grandparents had no choice but to rely on what was already present. When one neighbor didn't have food, my grandparents would invite them to share a meal.

No gifts go wasted. My granddad was an artist. He would take discarded materials and turn them into beautiful works of art. He saw people the same way. He always found the good in them.

Have parties and celebrate one another. I used to hear about the great parties behind my grandparents' housing project. They kept the tradition going after I was born. Every Friday, they held a gathering at their house, and people from the community would show up. My parents would often bring us along. I got to witness people celebrating their lives at the end of the week.

In the words of Mary Oliver, in her advice on living: "pay attention, be astonished, and tell about it." Her advice is my mantra. It embodies the practices and principles of the listener.

Disclaimer: don't waste people's time if you don't intend to use the gifts and talents you discover.

Paying Attention

Listening is more than asking survey questions or taking people at face value. On my first trips out in my formal role, I made some crucial mistakes.

First, I tried too hard to make what was natural into a job. The first house I visited was a family I grew to know.

Yusuf had a couple of sisters who lived across the street, several houses from the church, a half block down on Park. I remember the odd look on his sister's face when I asked about the gifts and talents they had. I explained that I was working for the church and the development corporation. I watched them shrink back, as if I had said something wrong. They were right.

There was an awkward silence, and after it, she sent me away. I tried the rest of the block and kept getting the same response.

It sucked being turned away.

I assumed abundance, even though the two organizations sharing my part-time salary had spent decades building services around needs.

I treated my neighbors as gifted people with a lot to offer, which was something they didn't expect.

My next mistake was not understanding that the community had been watching me long before I had a role. Plenty of people knew where I lived and knew I was a dad. I didn't realize my new neighbors were as curious about me as I was about them.

I failed to see the power of being a neighbor. Once I started introducing myself not as someone from the institutions but as a neighbor, the doors opened wide.

My survey was useless, because their gifts were right in front of my eyes. I went to Mike and said it wasn't working. I told him what had happened, and he told me to go back.

I went back, but this time I took Yusuf with me. He had already called his sister and explained what I was doing. This time I sat on their porch. I put away my survey and hung out.

Their porches were always full of family and neighbors. They would have serious conversations about who was good at what, and about what they deeply cared about. There was always food, and someone was always cooking.

They got to know me through Yusuf. They asked about my life and shared themselves with me, along with some neighborhood gossip. I started to learn that there was power in the ordinary, in being a neighbor, more valuable than any formal role.

Being a neighbor was a powerful currency. Most of all, their gifts were right in front of my face.

I had missed the healers in one house, the great cooks and entrepreneurs in another. I learned to truly listen, listen, listen. I learned to be present with all my senses. When those practices are in place, gifts are revealed. It reminded me that what I was listening for was abundance.

- Listen, listen, listen. The listener pays attention to what people do, not only what they say. (My son the scientist affirms this.)

- Notice, notice, notice. The listener hears who vouches for other people's gifts.
- Joy, joy, joy. The listener notices what brings people joy, and pays attention to the body language of people sharing it.
- Ask, ask, ask. The listener discovers gifts by holding beautiful questions, the kind that draw out passions: What is the accomplishment you are most proud of? What are you good enough to teach someone else? What brings you joy?

Being Astonished

Being astonished is like capacity building, but more effective. Being astonished is the act of celebrating what has been uncovered.

Since we weren't used to being treated as needed residents, with capacities and capital, we needed rituals to make gifts public. We did two things. One was to hold gatherings in a host's home, and every block had someone who loved to host.

As part of this social fabric, we had basic principles for institutions entering the space. I noticed that whenever an institution showed up, it automatically sucked the power out of the room.

So I created a practice. The institutions in the space could not offer opinions or solutions. The only way their representatives' voices could be heard was through clarifying questions about what they were hearing.

I went back to Yusuf's sister's house and asked them to host, and I paid for the meal. It ended up being a pitch-in with about 15 neighbors. Some knew one another, some were meeting for the first time. Also present were some members from our church, our development corporation, and other social service groups in the neighborhood.

You could see the residents were uncomfortable. During the icebreaker and introductions, a lot of guards were up. I stopped and explained the rule, and you could see the relief on the neighbors' faces that this was not about our institutions promising to fix our problems.

People went around the room, shared their passions, and talked about their dreams. It was refreshing to watch the surprise on people's faces as they got to know one another in a new way.

Akua's boyfriend talked about his love of photography and even brought his portfolio to show off. There was a lot of energy in the room. One woman said, "I'm a photographer too," and others asked whether she could do it as a service for them.

People were waiting to be asked what they could give. That public celebration mattered, because people bore witness to what the larger community of Indianapolis had ignored.

The other way we used ritual was on Sunday at the church, where we used worship to share gifts. With the development corporation, I would send the stories to a list of about 200 influencers.

- Be ready to bring people together informally to celebrate one another's gifts and to create witnesses for those gifts. This builds collateral with a neighbor.
- Cultivate institutional rituals that give a platform to local gifts in the larger community.
- Invest and inject social capital into the gifts you uncover. It is a sin to waste it.

Tell About It

A community's gifts must be seen and celebrated with delight and wonder. Every week, I would turn in stories of all the households I had visited.

They were short stories of each household and a summary of the block's gifts.

When they went out to the email list, I got overwhelming responses of surprise that all these gifts were present.

For example, I got a request from the development corporation to connect them with the neighbor who makes pies.

It was hard for folks from institutions to believe what we uncovered, as if the neighbors were from Mars. Most responded first by offering training to the neighbors, as if they didn't know how to do things. They could have led the training. Others were skeptical of the information. What surprised me most were the people who read the email, wanted to hire a neighbor, met them, and asked more curious questions of delight.

People from the institutions and from the neighborhood started recognizing that people had more to offer than their needs. It was the first time I helped my neighbors see the power of telling the stories of abundance.

This was connecting the epigenetics of joy between and across cultures.

There was also a ritual Broadway had started to build into its social fabric. As this change took place, my role started to look a little different.

Practices of Change

Building friendships and connections, or maybe I should say growing them, because it's more organic, is longer-term work than most people think.

It is truly 100-year work.

Jeremy Efroymson's foundation, and its desire to give money, needed the church to develop new practices.

The practices I was doing invited people to see something that had been invisible before.

We took the money, called the gardeners, and said, "We would like to give all 25 thousand dollars to you, to continue your work together." The gardeners wanted to know: what was the catch?

We explained that we wanted them in charge of the money, to do whatever they wanted, as long as it wasn't obscene or illegal. The other stipulation was that it couldn't carry the church's name. Last, the church wouldn't take any administrative fees.

This was important for the church to learn. Being a good neighbor meant changing its own practices too.

This change in practice changed how the church saw the neighborhood. Instead of thinking about what they could do for the neighborhood, they began to see their neighbors as gifted actors in the play of life. It revealed how stories about what people are passionate enough to get off the couch and do could shape real economic change for communities that are normally overlooked.

I continued this practice, and over two years about 800 thousand dollars came into our neighborhood. It went directly into the hands of the people who live there. Telling the stories of abundance is an act of stimulating an economy of gifts. It starts a revolution.

That was far more money than would have come before, and before, it would have gone overwhelmingly to the church, and there would have been much less of it. The gift economy would not have existed or survived.

- Once you begin to understand the gifts of your community, find ways to share what you learn with others.
- An institution has platform, social capital, and political capital that it can use to help community members share stories of their gifts.
- Connect people who have resources with people sharing their gifts in the community.

Scale vs. Multiplication

I started getting calls to share some of the practices we were using in our community around Broadway. I was invited to speak and lead workshops. I was even asked to scale this work by creating other Roving Listener programs.

Right now, there are 30-plus listening programs around the world. Most have struggled to start, or to get the same impact and learning we were having.

I never became the Roving Listener to have other people do this. I did it because I saw my grandparents thrive and live good lives by being good neighbors, giving people a place to stay when they needed one. They let no human gift go unwanted or wasted, and they understood the power of being needed.

I do this because one of my best friends dared to pay attention to what brought me joy. He listened to what I deeply cared about. He invested in my gift and connected me with people who helped me master my craft.

I do this because love and friendship let me know my gifts are needed, that I am needed. I hope those who are reading will not scale the Roving Listener but multiply the practices I have laid out. Follow Mary Oliver's advice on living: pay attention, be astonished, and tell about it.

Looking Ahead

In 2006, our family was looking to plant roots in the neighborhood near the church we attended. We were trying to buy a house. It was almost impossible to find one we could afford.

We packed our bags and bought a house just west of the neighborhood we had been in. As my work at Broadway was changing, Mike and I were holding questions. Does this work need structure or fabric? Could it be scaled? Mike would often say, "You can scale the construction of this church, but you can't scale people, because people aren't steel, or limestone, or concrete." The question for our community was how to multiply this, not scale it.

I would take these lessons, drawn from friends, stories, and faith, into the work of the Roving Listener in my new neighborhood, the Near Northwest neighborhood. I wanted to see whether the work around Broadway was isolated to that place.

I wanted to see whether I could take the fabric of the work cultivated there and apply it to my new neighborhood. Would it be possible, in this new place, to cultivate community, economy, and mutual delight?

Would the principles in practice reveal similar results? I wondered what we would discover, who would be involved, and what we would learn.

I was also curious, as I was getting calls to consult in other places. Could I really practice what I had been preaching?

I was concerned, because I didn't have the church as my anchor in the new neighborhood. I wasn't sure how it would work. We didn't yet know how important it was to be connected to a place that believed in us and saw us differently than others had before.

It was 2006, and I was maturing and growing in the practices of abundance.

The first opportunity came with my friend Anne Mitchell. We created a company called Tesserae Learning. Tesserae are the small pieces, often cubes, of glass, metal, ceramic, and stone used to make a mosaic.

We were taking the bits of a community, often discarded, and watching the beauty of the mosaic come alive before us.

Our mission was to figure out how community members, stakeholders, institutions, and associations could collaborate and learn together in ways that made our community better. We worked with institutions like the Arc of Indiana, the Commonwealth Disabilities Council of Kentucky, and the Council for Developmental Disabilities in Georgia, among others.

The work was good and satisfying. Yet working with institutions, government and nonprofit, made us even more aware of the challenges to real community flourishing. People still weren't seeing these communities as gifted. What could we do?

We did this work for a few years, and I wanted to do something rooted in the neighborhood, my neighborhood. I had this wild idea that my neighbors could be my business partners without putting in any money as equity, using their gifts instead, and committing to walk around with me and bear witness to the good things already happening in our neighborhood.

In return, I would share my consulting contracts with them, and they would commit to return 20 percent to a common pot we would use to give out our own local grants.

My neighbors were eager to do this. Even though no one called them philanthropists, they are. We agreed to call our new organism The Learning Tree. That's right, I named it after the tree my grandparents and their neighbors planted so the next generation would know the wisdom of the community and grow up with it.

We didn't know much about nonprofits, but we did this because we wanted to be good neighbors. A lot of other people wanted to do something for us, or for our neighborhood. We wanted to be witnesses to what was already happening. We wanted to celebrate and invest in that.

As we celebrated, as we failed and succeeded, as we kept taking steps forward, the road would take us places we never expected, across the world and in our own city and neighborhood.

CHAPTER 5

More Than a Five-Year Plan

Michael Mather

De'Amon's investment, literally and metaphorically, in his neighbors changed the way I imagined work could be done. I watched, not entirely from the sidelines, but I watched in wonder. As you could tell, it wasn't always easy, yet it did open the eyes of institutions in the larger community to the power of a community recognizing its own power and building from it.

My mother died twenty years ago (as I write these words). It's not 100 years. I was reminded this year how short those twenty years have been. 100 years doesn't look so long.

I was invited to the home of parishioners in South Bend. A friend of theirs, a nun from Africa, was visiting and they wanted us to meet.

After dinner our hosts asked the nun and me to tell the stories of our calls into the ministry.

I began telling them how I was in college, twenty-plus years earlier, in my late teens. I was a music major and I felt aware of being called into the ministry. I had a strong feeling of that, complete with a couple of signs of things that happened that affirmed my sense of call.

Then it was the nun's turn. She began, "Five hundred years ago. . . ."

She traced a story from her ancestors and from the land, leading to her call into the ministry.

I forgot my own story. I had forgotten all who had gone before me, whose lives and choices had made my way.

I can be shortsighted. I don't read the signs of the times, the signs of all that has gone before that has brought us to this moment.

When there is pushback on learning the whole story of the history of this country, it is easy to point out the practices of forgetting have been deeply rooted in our culture for a very long time.

There was a woman in my congregation in Indianapolis. When I left in 2020 she was over 100 years old. She had known her grandfather, who had been held in slavery in this country. I was one person removed from knowing someone who was held in slavery. It wasn't as long ago as I had often thought.

Having a sense of perspective, an accurate sense of perspective, is not an easy thing to have in our culture. Every generation thinks the current generation is lazier or more challenged, or different from theirs. We find it easy to think ourselves as different from one another, failing to realize our commonality. Making short-term or long-term plans for the future, doing it without an accurate sense of perspective or time, is not going to serve us well. In fact, it hasn't.

Over the last twenty years I have traveled around this country talking with many organizations, mainly religious congregations (of all stripes), but also with social service organizations and government organizations.

These groups will often show me their strategic plans. Most of them are ten- to twenty-year plans. Some of them are shorter.

They are short on imagination and long on planning.

De'Amon told me about his visit with a First Nations group in Canada to consult. He got up and said he was there to help build community. The chief interrupted and said, "No, we are here to remember community."

Strategic plans are often very good ideas for constructing buildings. It's essential to have the right measurements and to understand the physics of buildings. Such strategic planning can be good for human organizations and communities, but only if deeply rooted in remembering community.

Knowing the story, the epigenetics of joy, in one's own community is the only ground from which real healing can grow.

Community is not the same thing as building an office building, monument, or school. Building community doesn't work with steel, lumber, nails, or any other type of building material.

The building materials of communities are human beings. And human beings aren't steel. There are different tools needed for the different kinds of building we are talking about.

Using the same process for building a skyscraper that we use for healing a community just doesn't work. It might be nice if it did, but it doesn't.

My own experience is in talking with congregations who are fighting dwindling resources, and smaller numbers of members (I mean "members" in the broadest sense of the word), and who believe they can plan their way out of the crises in which they live.

When we sit around and talk history/tell stories though, that is when things come alive.

"How did this food pantry start at your church?" Very rarely does someone say, "Well we did a strategic plan fifty years ago and it was item number seven on our list." They say, Joshua and Shaunte felt like it was important and they started doing it.

Ah . . . there is something to learn. 100 year work, or 500 year work, starts with something born in the passion and commitment of the people who are part of the community.

It doesn't often happen by either vote *or* consensus. It happens by energy. And that energy drives the practice.

Trusting the energy is truly an act of faith. If we follow the evidence of what hasn't been working for us, it shouldn't have to take us very far to begin saying to ourselves: "Hmm, maybe taking a different route might get us to a new destination."

I was talking with a historian who told me the right questions, the ones that elicit stories from our histories, often help us have difficult conversations about racism.

If you begin by saying "How are you going to take on being anti-racist?" defensiveness appears quickly.

If you ask, "During the civil rights movement, what role did your church or people in your church play?" People tell stories, and they begin to form the imagination to remember where they want to go or *don't* want to go and what they want to do or what they don't want to do.

These are the ways of trusting the stories, the epigenetics of joy, at work in all kinds of institutions: philanthropies, government, social services, businesses, and even religious communities!

This made sense to me. After nearly ten years of ministry, a member of my congregation challenged me, and I turned things on their head. Instead of asking people who came to the food pantry, "Tell us how poor you are; how needy you are" we changed the question to "Ttell us how gifted you are? Have you taken care of children? Do you play a musical instrument, cook for more than ten people, do drywall?"

The question we asked gave us completely different answers. It was (for the first time) useful information, not just information we hadn't looked for before. The church needed people to need us. And we were blind to the fact of the people who came seeking food were needing to be needed.

They were giving us an opportunity to discover something we hadn't known was therewhen all we were interested in seemed to be what was wrong with people.

A few years after we started asking people what they were good at, I remember being really surprised when this guy told us he was great at making cheese. I hadn't paid much attention. But a woman who was sitting with me followed up with him and soon discovered he was a master cheesemaker and he was making cheese in his basement on stainless steel equipment, kept immaculately clean.

I was often acting in the presence of the person appearing before me asking for some food or emergency assistance. If I did, it took me a long time to learn I was going to miss a lot of good stuff.

When we act like we *only* live in the present, we are leaving unused gospel lying all around (from Willie James Jennings in his book *After Whiteness*).

This is my central concern. I am leaving unused gospel lying all around. When I don't recognize all there is to "play with" (as De'Amon loves to say), I am missing the exalted possibilities there are in each moment.

After a few years of asking people their gifts at the food pantry, we had what we called "The Soul Liberation Festival" on the street outside of our church in South Bend.

We didn't know what we were doing except we knew we wanted to celebrate all we were discovering. We invited the people who had come to our food pantry: carpenters, artists, musicians, pipe fitters, accountants, athletes, entrepreneurs. We had a party.

It was energy. It reminded us, and showed us, who we are in all our rich diversity. It is hard to hold on to such a thing in a country always hardening between our differences and wringing our hands about them. Maybe the way out of some of the morass we get into is to have parties for no apparent reason.

Maybe simply getting together to celebrate and have a good time is an excellent five-year plan. After five years of parties what did we learn? What new gifts did we discover?

The other night a relatively new friend invited some new and old friends to come together for a party. I had no idea these folks could prepare a feast, a table full of foods representing different cultures from the families around the table. There were thoughtful gifts, chosen with each person in mind. Meticulously wrapped gifts. These people need to be in charge of celebrations!

If we keep exploring, learning about each other, new possibilities will break in upon us. And I hope we will be wise enough to both sit with these gifts and then figure out what we'll try next in building on what we have, not on what we don't have.

In 2017, five days before Christmas, a fire broke out in the lower level of the church I served in Indianapolis. It was devastating. The poinsettias in the sanctuary were dulled by the gray ashes settled on the red leaves.

Chairs and tables melted. It looked like the hellscape from some postapocalyptic movie set.

Unable to gather in the sanctuary on Christmas Eve, we stuffed ourselves into the chapel, with a huge fan rumbling trying to pull the smoke out as we gathered and bellowed Christmas carols above the sounds of the turbines.

As awful as the fire was, it gave the church our future. We imagined in ways we hadn't before, when a lot of problems were literally burned away. Old electric wiring had to be replaced with wiring now up to code. We had to make new choices. It took us several years and millions of dollars from our insurance company, but we imagined spaces in and around the building in new ways.

We had t-shirts made about "re-igniting." Perhaps you might consider that to be dangerous, but not nearly as dangerous as the intern who 6 months prior to the fire had "Arsonist of the Spirit" tattooed onto the back of her neck! And then had to live with it when the fire happened!

Re-igniting was a way for us to take the destructive force and say "what are we noticing we hadn't noticed before?" For 6 months or more we had scaffolding up above the chandeliers hanging above the congregation. You could walk on the platform to the stained glass above the balcony and look at the work up close and personal. We looked at ourselves up close and personal. We looked at our neighbors up close and personal. We re-designed the community room downstairs and re-branded it updating it dramatically not only for church gatherings but for others in the community at large. So many of our neighbors, some of whom had not set foot in our building, came over to say: "how can we help?"

Our present, before the fire, was blocking me from seeing possibilities before us. I remember the old story about the sculptor who was asked how she creates a statue. She said, "I simply cut away the parts not belonging to the statue." I was seeing a new world because a part of the old one was burned away.

The present structures had blinded me to the possibilities waiting to be born. The fire, as terrible as it was, was a gift.

How can I clear out my old way of thinking without burning it all down? How can I see the unused gospel lying around without destroying the things getting in the way for me to see?

100 years work into the future, involves remembering that 100 years work also is behind us, holding us up, challenging us, embarrassing us, causing us to dream new dreams.

People talk a lot these days about being present for one another. Being present for one another means really paying attention.

When I moved to Boulder, early in the pandemic in 2020, there were a lot of people who live on the streets of Boulder who hung out on the patio of the church I am serving.

This was a new thing to me. In the neighborhoods in which I had lived and worked for thirty-five years, there was a lot of "couch surfing." People who didn't have a place to live would find friends or family who would welcome people to their home for brief or extended stays while the person dealt with whatever challenge lay ahead of them.

We weren't meeting in person at the church so there weren't a lot of comments to me about the people hanging out on the porch. When we started, slowly and carefully, to meet in person for a few things, folks in the church asked me to tell people to leave the porch.

I thought about it. It seemed like too easy a solution. *And* it didn't really solve anything. So I said to the people who came to me, "I won't kick them off the porch, but if you want to, you can kick them off the porch. But before you do that you must learn their names."

I didn't know what to do. I had come to know many of the people hanging out on the porch. I knew one man who has lived on the streets of Boulder for over eleven years.

When I asked him what he had learned over those eleven years his response astonished me: "Mike, this is the most stress-free life I have ever had." This was not what I expected.

One of the leaders of the church asked if I could set up a meeting between people in the congregation and people who hang out on the porch, who live on the streets.

I was happy to do it.

We had five people from the porch and five people from the congregation gather in the parlor of the church, socially distanced of course.

We went around the circle and I asked everyone to give their first name and then to share something that brings them joy.

When we finished the introductions there had been information that people wanted to follow up on ("Oh, you're from Lancaster, Pennsylvania; I've spent time out there!" or "Oh, you're a new grandparent, I'm a new parent!").

After another half an hour of conversation I turned to the people in the congregation and asked, "Is there anything you wanted to say to these folks who are hanging out on the porch?"

The surprising response, "no," came back.

When we trusted and brought people together for what all expected to be a "hard conversation" it in fact became a conversation overflowing with joy, imagination, and connection.

Three years later we hired a couple of people we met from the porch, who are good listeners and good at discernment, if they would take a (well-paid) part-time job identifying the gifts, talents, dreams, and passions of their neighbors.

Good planning often means having conversations we hadn't thought about having before. When I wrote in chapter 2 about the conversation that a corporation brought together about ending poverty there was a surprising (and embarrassing to me) revelation.

Over the course of our introductions to one another, we discovered that most of the twelve to fifteen people in this conversation were also part of religious congregations of one sort or another.

De'Amon picked up on it and asked the people in the conversation if they had ever had this conversation (about ending poverty) as part of the conversation around their community of faith.

Not one person reported such a conversation. What does it say to us that it is more likely for a private corporation to have this conversation than a religious community, some of whose members are engaged with this conversation at their workplace.

I was very impressed with the people who were giving themselves to this conversation. They clearly were very committed to this subject. In many cases their whole lives were engaged with this subject through one lens or another. Yet not one of the religious communities of which they were a part had invited or encouraged such a conversation. Good energy being wasted.

Good planning takes a good foundation. And the people from the congregation and the people who live on the street now have the beginning of a relationship on which to build whatever comes from this if we decide to take this next step.

Planning is not primarily adopting a process, it's opening up relationships that can help us dream new dreams. My friendships with De'Amon and Seana have changed my life and have caused me to look at the world differently. This didn't come about through a strategic planning process.

Part of it is leaving aside some of our old expectations and ways of thinking. After the meeting between people hanging out on the patio and folks from the congregation one of the staff people from the congregation came to me with excitement!

"Mike, I have an idea!" I was looking forward to hearing her idea. "Amazon lockers!" she said. "What do you mean?" I asked. "We could get Amazon lockers here at the church for people on the street to keep their stuff in and it would be safe."

This is one of the challenges we all have, wanting to fix things. I asked the person from our staff: "Who asked you to fix this?"

She looked at me: "What do you mean?" I said, "No one asked us to fix anything." "But I like to fix things!" she said. Indeed. Me too.

Later someone else would come say almost the exact same thing to me and this staff person (the Amazon lockers idea). She said to this person, "You know, I was thinking the same thing. The more I think about it I think we should go back and have a conversation and listen for the clues to what the people who live on the streets are already doing and what they are learning about it and see if we can support their idea."

She went on, "It may not be as good an idea as our Amazon locker idea, but if it's their idea, they will get closer to the solution that will probably be *even better* than our Amazon locker idea."

Ah, I remember thinking, "teach me." I was learning a lot as I listened to her.

Part of 100 year work is developing the relationships to take us past our savior complexes and more deeply into relationship. We can build something new and strong together if we can give up the idea we are fixing the other person in this relationship (as a pastor who has met across the years with many couples having difficulty, I can say confidently "I'm going to fix you and then our relationship will work" isn't very effective).

Instead, if we really listen, we can discover new possibilities from which to build. A few minutes later one of the church members from the meeting stopped in and said, "Mike, I think I know Sam." (Sam was one of the people hanging out on the porch, who had come to the gathering.) "What do you mean?" I asked.

She went on, "I think I know his dads. I think he grew up in my neighborhood, but it's been a very long time since I've seen him. When I go home tonight I'm going to go talk with them."

She later came back to me and told me it was the person she remembered who grew up in her neighborhood. And his dads didn't know where he was.

When we really listen and pay attention we can make plans for the most important work there is, waiting to be born. Perhaps it is healing just waiting to arrive.

It's very much like we don't notice or remember the things that have fed our lives for the better. I can easily forget how most of the success that has come to me has come because people loved and accepted me even when I've done really dumb things.

When I was voted on to be a member of the clergy of The United Methodist Church, I often responded very aggressively and counter to the prevailing wisdom and rules of the church in those days. So why did I succeed?

My father was a respected member of the United Methodist clergy in Indiana. I recognize now what I never could have acknowledged then: I was ordained because people said, "Well, he's Herb Mather's son. He seems a little crazy, but Herb's all right, so he probably will be too."

We have an Alzheimer's problem as a culture, and I am still trying to overcome my own. Our society doesn't remember who we are anymore. We don't recognize our own history, our own story, our own herstory. We try to hide it, like the truth won't set us free, but hurt us.

I think of this often when we talk about immigration in this country, failing to realize that overwhelmingly most of us are immigrants to this country.

In Exodus, God reminds the Hebrew people fleeing slavery who have now come to a new land, a new home. God wants them to think about how they welcome the stranger: "You were once immigrants in the land of Egypt" (Exodus 22:21 CEB).

Without a sense of history we won't meet strangers and make friends, we will meet strangers and make enemies. The plans we make for enemies are different from the plans we make for friends.

Recently I read a book by a doctor in Indiana called *Canary in the Coal Mine*. The young doctor talks about making plans for a community center in the rural, small-town community where he lives and practices.

A local official embezzled the money and disappeared.

Heartbroken, the doctor goes on a mission trip to Latin America. He visits a place where they are celebrating the opening of a community center.

One of the locals in that place tells the doctor that he and another friend were planning this for the last twenty-five years.

What took so long, the doctor wanted to know.

Well, the reply came, for the first twenty years nothing happened and then five years ago, it did!

Patience.

When I lived in Indianapolis the neighborhood around me was gentrifying. As the pastor of a church in the neighborhood I often got calls from new residents and journalists asking me if I was interested in being part of a conversation about "good gentrification."

I usually told them no. If they asked why I told them. I'm busy *and* as much attention as is going to be paid to the gentrification—in the media in conversations in the neighborhood organization, etc—what is not talked about is what is happening to people who had lived for more than one generation in that neighborhood and are being forced out.

A large number of low-income citizens and neighbors were moving out to the far east side of Indianapolis. When I went to visit them in their new homes, I noticed things I often noticed in the neighborhood where I lived and worked—before the reinvestment from gentrification.

There were cracked and buckled sidewalks. Pools of water in the street though it hadn't rained in weeks.

Some in my congregation told me they remembered when Black folks started moving into the neighborhood around Broadway and the white folks began to flee. They talked about the struggles and the argument and the fights happening in the congregation in those years. Painful memories for a lot of people. People who stayed and people who left.

In the 1950s and 1960s they had plans about how to stop white flight. None of which were successful. They had battles over accepting or not accepting the new Black faces, which were beginning to occasionally walk through the church doors on Sunday morning.

If the planning decision had been less about how to keep this from happening and more about discovering what is going on and learning from that and trying some things out, rather than putting all of our eggs in one basket, it would have been, perhaps, a bit less painful.

I reached out to the United Methodist churches in the east side where my parishioners and neighbors were moving, I reached out to the district superintendent, I reached out to the bishop and I said, "You know the same thing is happening to the east side that happened in the neighborhood around Broadway back in the 1950s, 1960s and 1970s. There are people from our congregation who lived through those times. We would be happy to talk with people from the congregations on the east side and tell them all the mistakes we made."

The inquiry met with silence. The churches out on the east side, and their leaders, didn't think the same thing that happened to Broadway would happen to them. I understand.

For decades I have signed up for or convened conversations that aren't asking the big picture question, but only the small one.

If we know the gifts of the people around us we think we are serving, those gifts can become the building blocks of any future we imagine.

Discovery—learning both what we don't know, and what we already know—is important.

Not being aware of what is around us, what is present, won't lead us anywhere.

On the issue of gentrification I remember wondering if we work on the property tax policy if that would change the future? A Jesuit economist from Chicago assured me it wouldn't.

Whether it would or wouldn't wasn't the answer. I was looking at things the wrong way. I could have brought people together who were being moved out to the east side with people who I knew living out on the east side and see what grew out of those conversations.

De'Amon's challenge to me was to find ways to have policy built on abundance, rather than on ideas (even the really cool ideas I had). So how do we do that?

What is the conversation we could have that would change the continual shifting of chairs on the *Titanic*?

It's not that I didn't care about the gentrifying area. All the attention is focused on that community. I wanted to be part of a different conversation. A deeper conversation about all the people.

Those conversations are hard to find.

At my new church in Boulder, Colorado, I came across the same type of thing. As I noted, there are a lot of people who live on the streets of Boulder.

There is also, for the middle class and working poor, an affordability issue in Boulder. "Affordable housing" starts around $350,000. Not particularly "affordable."

A school teacher, a wise soul, in our church cares deeply about these issues. He teaches in a school system miles away, full of students from low-income, low-wealth families.

He wonders if we could turn the church building into a few units of affordable housing.

I love he is excited by this. I wonder if we could think bigger.

We have abundance avoidance. We lay aside this social capital we have, to do something smaller, less effective, than if we dream about real change.

It's not an either/or question. We can do both, if we can keep reminding ourselves of the story. We can also learn from what we have done wrong.

We can try to be humble and keep thinking about what we can learn about these intractable problems. Discovery and learning are just other ways to say "Let's go on an adventure together. We don't know where it will lead. We know we are committed to one another and to wherever our exploration leads us together."

Recently the chair of trustees (sort of the building committee) at my church in Boulder has gotten shirts and hats made for the people on her committee.

The shirts and hats read "First Church Trustees—50 year fix!"

I love it. What exactly are they going to do? They don't know yet, but they are committed to figuring it out together.

I'm thinking maybe I can get shirts made saying: "First Church Boulder: Exploring 50- to 100-years Fixes! Join us!"

We're taking a learning journey in a few weeks to talk with people in Washington, DC, and Baltimore about housing. There are people going from our church and from our larger community. There are young people going. There are older people going. We are committed to discovering things together. We don't know where it will lead us, but we are pleased to go on this trip together.

Do we have the attention span for these conversations? Do we have the imagination?

Frederick Douglass did. W. E. B. Dubois did. Sojourner Truth did. Can we?

In De'Amon's next chapter you will see how his work in his local community began to be noticed throughout the larger community. It started in small ways via parties, and connections, and friendships. It is what always changes us for the good.

CHAPTER 6

Cultivating Joy to Create a Strong Fabric

De'Amon Harges

In 2016, Mike Mather and I took what would be our final learning journey with John McKnight. For many years, John had a cabin in Spring Green, Wisconsin. It was a getaway for family and friends, and one of the places celebrated in the Green Book for its use of community assets.

It is the place where the great architect Frank Lloyd Wright created Taliesin, a home of design and structure and, I would say, fabric. Frank's work and design teach.

When John invited us, we asked him what his agenda was. He said learning, friendship, and joy were the only aim. Mike and I replied, "It sounds like our type of fun."

John's big question was similar to Mike's question about multiplication in my last chapter. John's question was rooted in evolution over centuries. He was asking what his late friend, the social theorist Ivan Illich, had asked: How do we cultivate the fabric for abundance over 100 years?

I was spending a lot of time thinking about the role of an institution in this framework, this fabric. We arrived in Spring Green in the early afternoon and walked into town. Our conversations were about joy, and the culture of joy.

Mike talked about always finding ways to explore and learn in new places. He was so excited about learning how people live. He also talked about his joy in books. I talked about the joy of throwing parties, being at parties and celebrations, and watching people have fun. John talked a lot about jazz and playing cards with his friends.

We had a late snack and sat at the table while John told us stories about his adventures with his friend Ivan Illich, starting with the days of CIDOC (Centro Intercultural de Documentacion). John reveled in the celebrations that would happen at CIDOC.

John told us stories of things he learned and experienced there. He was slowly moving like a jazz riff into a conversation about how hospitality is the structure of belonging. This is where I started to think more clearly about the social archetypes for a beloved community.

You can tell it brought John much joy to explore new things with his friends, even at the age of 90. The last day there we went out to visit Taliesin even though John had been there several times before. It was like being there with him for the first time.

John shared his joy for the things he had learned about this place. I was amazed by the way that being curious brought John joy. Afterward, we headed into town for lunch. We started reflecting about our day, and how much joy there was in being together, learn together, and have meals together.

I wondered aloud with John what his next move would be. John relaxed in his chair and said with a slight grin, "Well, I am looking to describe the fabric of an abundant community. What holds it together? What practices promote associational life . . . *together*! Who are the people, and what are their roles in welcoming the stranger to this beloved community?"

John got me to think about structure versus fabric, systems versus culture. Fabric and culture were closer to what I was getting at. The questions

John was exploring changed how I looked at those same questions in my own community.

Mike and I would have many walks and talks—mostly in Indianapolis, but also across the country—on this subject. It helped us see that what we were talking about was social fabric, not some architectural plans to build a power plant.

We can replicate brick and mortar. It's easy to predict. We can build systems for that, but it's a lot harder to do the same with people. We are so diverse; no two people are exactly alike. We are fallible, beautiful, and ugly all at the same time.

There are no best practices, no textbook, and no magic pill in a beloved community. It's just the fabric of belonging, love, joy, and faith. It is a flexible tapestry of all of us sharing what we have and, more importantly, who we are.

What is in the fabric of an abundant community?

What practices help precipitate life together in a beloved community?

Who are the actors and their roles that help welcome the stranger?

Who holds the edge and the center closely?

How do we get people to fall in love with one another?

There are other questions that are relevant but to me these are at the base and are most important to hold.

PAY ATTENTION, BE ASTONISHED, AND TELL ABOUT IT!

It's good to be seen at a hip hop Cypher!

By 2016, The Learning Tree team had deepened its roots in the UNWA (United NorthWest Area) community. We had many more neighbors and had uncovered more gifts in people. We had a few learning journeys under our belts, and we were really getting to know one another in ways that bonded us across all our currencies (trust, love, imagination), tangible and intangible.

Together, we all wanted people from our neighborhood to be seen and regarded as beautiful right now and not something that needed to be made beautiful or fixed.

Most people from the outside saw the abandoned houses and empty lots as an eyesore and blight. We saw a blank canvas to show off our beauty, gifts, and culture.

Some of my neighbors—Fernando Rodriguez, Tysha Ahmed, Wildstyle Paschall, Amanda Wolf—along with myself and others started an art installation series called Cultivating Joy, using photographs that Wildstyle and other photographers took of neighbors using their gifts: being good parents, loving their children, creating art.

We had these photographs blown up to six feet by six feet or bigger. They told the stories of abundance in our community. We put them up on abandoned houses and empty lots, then threw parties and celebrations in front of or on the properties we had curated.

We were learning that what I had experienced in the fabric at Broadway with Mike and Seana could translate in similar ways to the community. We were making the invisible visible. We were putting on the abandoned homes and buildings what was already happening in the streets and homes of our neighborhood.

What we learned was for people to belong they first must be seen, seen as whole people. Next, people need to be celebrated in the public square. If there isn't a public square, create one by finding people who love hosting. Use abandoned homes and buildings. As Mike often says: "tell the story."

The first abandoned house we curated was right across the street from my house. It had been empty for several years. It seemed in perfect condition from the outside, but no one lived there. It had no life, only tall, seedy grasses that somehow hinted at what could be.

When we put the photographs up and cut the grass and planted some flowers, people would drive or walk by and stop in their tracks to investigate.

When I saw this, I suggested to my team—mostly as a friendly competition—that we hire our teenage neighbor to hang out with a clicker counter, count how many people stopped by, and listen to what they said.

The first week more than twenty-five people stopped and admired the exhibit. Over half the people my young neighbor would encounter would talk about their gifts, talents, and dreams. They would share what they would want people to see about them. The beautiful thing was that there were no words on the exhibit, and people knew what it was. It was evidence that people were starving to belong and needed witnesses and accomplices with them and their gifts.

We started thinking of what we could do that would bring people together to have a joyful time without being all preachy but at the same time bring a sense of communion in public.

My neighbor, Wildstyle, is a hip hop producer and is well-known around the city for his eye for talent. He suggested hosting a Hip Hop Cypher. These are poets, vocalists, and wordsmiths getting together in a circle to display their verbal skills. It's mostly done as a friendly competition with beats and music created by different producers. Wildstyle put the call out for artists. About twenty-five people signed up to participate.

We also made a few rules: all the words had to be about joy and celebration, and we would open with a ritual. The morning of the event, excitement was buzzing on our block. Neighbors asked what time it started and whether they could bring anything. We told them to bring themselves and their joy. We knew not everyone participating was Christian or went to church, but we asked Mike Mather to bless the ceremony.

We knew Mike was really good at convening celebrations, creating the words that set the environment for people to fall in love with one another.

At the beginning he said some words and then he prayed and then everyone cheered. He was the only white guy there with around fifty folks gathered and crowded around the house that was once empty with tall grass, now a finely curated artwork that celebrated the people who lived around it. It was a place that reminded people that they were children of God.

Our next exhibit happened on the corner of Rader and 26th Street, a few blocks away but with the same spirit. There were two buildings: one an empty house, the other a two-story apartment building.

One of the things most misunderstood about our neighborhood is education and how our neighbors feel about it. Because we are a low-wealth community, people would blame us for low test scores and failing neighborhood schools. It was said—in conversation and in news reports—that the reason our community was poorly educated was that parents didn't care about their children's education. So the answer was to run programs around education and bring in schools with the expertise to create better ones. Most were implemented through charter systems. It contradicted the research about why schools were important. The real reason was to raise property values, which mattered most to the residents currently living in that community.

It also attracted new money and opportunity to a neighborhood, which is not bad in itself, but it wasn't truthful. It didn't create trust, because it undermined the real experts.

Our friend Seana teaches us that parents are the first teachers. The other contradiction was that it wasn't that people didn't believe in education. Many were working two jobs, contending with the housing conditions in our neighborhood and with banks unwilling to loan us money because of the narratives about our people.

The sad thing is that the investments made in new schools in our community, time after time—especially at the historic School 42—were rooted in stories from the past. I had connections to the school through friends from church who had taught there. For decades, School 42 became a focus of the school corporation every year. So much so that in the neighborhood we joked, "Oh, this is the new school of the week." We all knew they were going to try something new on us without ever talking to us. We decided to counter-protest.

The claims that we didn't care about education in our neighborhood caused us to curate an exhibition we called "Community as School."

We used an abandoned building directly across the street from School 42. We walked around our neighborhood with cameras, and Wildstyle photographed neighbors teaching one another, formally and informally.

There was a young man teaching people how to fix bicycles. There was a mother teaching her children and her neighbor's children, painting on canvas. We blew up the photographs and put them on that abandoned building right across the street from that school, celebrating members of our community as teachers.

Teachers would walk in that school being reminded that the parents were the first teachers of their students!

My friends Daryl and Stephanie Answer who live in Kansas City, Missouri, have a similar project. Young people in their neighborhood go around and ask their neighbors: "What are you good enough to teach someone else how to do and would you be willing to show others what you know?"

They call their school project Eastside University where their community reveals itself as a campus, each house becomes a classroom, and every person is a teacher. Learning from that, we didn't need more specialized classrooms, we needed more specialized listeners of abundance.

We did a few more of these projects, which led to us being seen as a community with lots of gifts and currencies, even without a lot of money. It gave us a lot to think about as we turned to creating social fabric. We now had people coming to hang out with us from outside the neighborhood.

Nearby Marian University started holding writing classes on the front porches of neighbors. The neighbors became co-teachers with the professors. Sister Norma, a nun at Marian University at the time, was a liberation theologian and practitioner.

Sister Norma would join us, along with students and professors, for meals in our house—no agenda, just love in conversation. People came in as strangers and left as friends and accomplices. Mary Oliver's words of advice on living remind me of the practices of the gospel.

- Pay attention: to find abundance, you have to look for it—not to hoard capital, but to look for it in people and their gifts.
- Be astonished: be curious about your neighbor, and curious about how they might be needed in your life and in the lives of others.
- Tell about it: be a witness to the goodness in the world and in yourself. Where you see God working, share it in the public square—celebrate it in worship, in your congregation, or by throwing a party at your house for someone else.

Fishes and Loaves: Multiplying from Community Listeners to Community Ambassadors

In 2017, The Learning Tree had become pretty well known, not only in Indianapolis but around the country, for loving to throw parties. We had progressed from throwing parties ourselves to supporting people who would throw their own, like Rowe and Earl.

Rowe and Earl are a young couple who offered violin lessons, tutoring, and snacks on their front porch after school. They organized our first Open Bite Night. What is Open Bite Night? Rowe and Earl invited their neighbors to cook food, set a table in the street, and offer their dishes for sale and tasting—an abundance festival!

Another neighbor, Januarie York, known for her salon-style meals called "Bread," hosted house concerts and front-porch conversations way before it was popular. We took what we already knew and made it part of our fabric. It remains part of our fabric.

We had a few rules for people coming from outside our neighborhood:

- Come curious about people's gifts.
- The agenda is friendship—hopefully you leave in love with someone new.

- Don't project your power over people; instead, ask questions that provoke curiosity about abundance.
- Be vulnerable.

We had a reputation for parties. People around the country would call to bear witness to what others had told them about coming to a party in our neighborhood. When people visited us from around the country—we were getting well known—we would throw a party or send them to neighbors' homes to visit and share a meal.

One group from Memphis and Nashville asked, "Why would people have us, strangers, into their homes?" We replied, "Because they are our neighbors, and we asked."

In Indianapolis, we got connected with our local community foundations, the Central Indiana Community Foundation and the Indianapolis Foundation. They had just finished research on how to become a more equitable institution—one that creates an environment where citizens who are often forgotten or unseen get the opportunity to live to their full potential, no matter their race, place, or identity.

Mike and I had a long relationship with the then-president and CEO of the Central Indiana Community Foundation (CICF), Brian Payne. Brian would often come to parties and dinners with my neighbors.

He was learning from his experience with neighbors and the work we were doing around Broadway Church.

Brian started throwing parties and inviting his friends and our neighbors to participate in gatherings at his house. The work of the Roving Listener and the evolution of The Learning Tree would influence what would become the Indianapolis Foundation/CICF ambassadors.

The new mission challenged the foundation to lean heavily on relationships and shared power.

The community foundation knew that in order for people to build trust they would have to invest time to cultivate authentic meaningful relationships with Indianapolis residents.

It became clear to the foundation that they needed people who already had the currency of trust—people who saw others for their gifts and saw possibilities in every problem. The foundation started with close to thirty-five people all over Indianapolis to listen to community members' dreams and passions. They also listened for where people were already acting, with agency, to solve community problems.

I got a call from my neighbor Rob MacPherson, who is also the vice president of community strategy for the foundation. He asked if I would participate—it would be good to have me involved to give guidance and support, because of the work I did as the Roving Listener. (I had met Rob by knocking on his door while roving in our neighborhood.)

I admit I was pretty skeptical, borderline jaded, that a philanthropic institution was interested in being a good neighbor. That same institution, not long before, had turned us down for a grant because our project budget was too big and our operating budget was too small. (We didn't have an operating budget, or a building, or paid employees.) We were penalized for being volunteers.

The foundation wanted to hire people from around the city—calling them "ambassadors"—to be roving listeners in their own communities. Of course, the people chosen would be people who were already listeners in their communities.

I decided to explore a relationship with the foundation if the rest of the Learning Tree team was up for it.

As we began this partnership with the foundation, we became aware it would be helpful to name the archetypes we identified as strongly serving this work.

A Community Ambassador embodies the following archetypes and characteristics:

Philanthropic by Nature: A Community Ambassador possesses a spirit of generosity and service. They contribute their time, talents, and resources without expectation of personal gain, focusing instead on the well-being of others and the community as a whole.

Connector: A Community Ambassador believes that meaningful relationships are the foundation for solving community challenges. They cultivate and leverage social capital to connect individuals, organizations, and resources. They freely share their networks and opportunities in order to build stronger connections and communities.

Person Centered: A Community Ambassador intentionally builds relationships with individuals and groups who are often overlooked, underrepresented, or marginalized. They seek to understand people's strengths and needs and actively work to ensure that everyone has opportunities to participate in community life.

Abundance Centered: A Community Ambassador believes in the beloved community and that all people are welcome. They focus on opportunities rather than deficits and organize people around their strengths and assets. Rather than simply identifying problems, they generate ideas, mobilize resources, and help create solutions.

Truth Tellers: A Community Ambassador demonstrates courage and integrity by speaking honestly about challenges and inequities within the community. They are willing to engage in respectful disagreement while remaining committed to constructive solutions. They elevate stories of individuals and groups who are taking action, and they rely on facts, evidence, and lived experience to inform and support their advocacy.

The first listening sessions were fun. We used the walls of an abandoned building to create a visual asset map, where ambassadors named the hopes, dreams, and gifts their neighbors were contributing to the neighborhood. We had a neighborhood artist illustrate, with paint and drawing, what they were saying.

Pam Boss Ross

Pam Ross had just been promoted to a new position created to explore this work: vice president of equity and inclusion at the Central Indiana Community Foundation (CICF). We started out as eight residents, from eight different neighborhoods—always overlooked, unseen, and undervalued.

We represented neighborhoods that were seen as "needy" and treated as invisible all around the city. Pam's role with us was to help us cultivate an organic fabric for the community ambassadors project.

While driving with my neighbor Wildstyle to our first gathering as ambassadors, I was telling him how I don't believe institutions can be good neighbors. He replied, "I know, but I think this is a chance to take what we've been cultivating and guide them through a process. I don't want to see them take our work and extract it for the wrong reasons."

When we got in the room we sat down quietly.

Neighbors were there: Beatrice, Annie, and a few more folks, including Pam Ross. Pam was just starting her job at the foundation. This would be an introduction for all of us.

I brought no agenda and made it clear I just wanted to get to know who each of the ambassadors were, as people. Pam has presence. You know when she is in the room, even when she isn't saying anything. She's authentic and straight to the point.

We sat for two hours and talked and got to know one another. It was a good time. I think all of us left there knowing we were glad to meet one another, but we were all still skeptical. A lifetime of being treated badly or even invisibly by institutions wouldn't be erased in an afternoon.

We met regularly over the next six months. Pam, in her new job as vice president of the foundation, got a lot of pressure from Brian to come up with something concrete about the Ambassadors to guide the institution.

Brian thought this was going to be a program initiative, a product for Pam and her official role with the foundation. Pam knew what we all knew: that the biggest part of our work is friendship, joy, and care for one another. In other words, love.

Ambassadors were a little protective of our communities and the people in them. This caused us to bombard Pam with questions—hard questions, very pointed questions, very critical questions about the community foundation and its motives.

We asked questions like "what are you going to do about specific problems and if we find possibilities are you going to actually invest in those possibilities?"

Questions, questions, questions. Question after question, Pam responded with honesty: she didn't know if the community foundation really wanted to learn from us and our neighbors.

This built trust. She answered our questions the best she could. She took time to deeply pay attention to the stories of the Ambassadors and their neighbors. Pam as a person embodied what it meant for institutions to become good neighbors. Leadership makes a difference.

Pam Ross kept getting pressure for how the Ambassadors were going to function in and out of the foundation from Brian, but Pam continued to push back.

It had been six and a half months before our first official meeting with the community foundation. We would become part of the all-staff meetings at the foundation once a month.

I remember listening to the ambassadors introduce themselves and why we were here and what we were here for. The ambassadors celebrated Pam and her listening. They celebrated her practice, and they went to bat for her. One of the Ambassadors, Valerie Davis, said, "For this work to be done, the people in power must give up their power and listen. The reason we are at the table is because Pam has done that."

Brian was taken aback by the ambassadors' support for Pam. And he was struck by the ambassadors naming the practices of abundance, starting with relationship first.

We put together a contract. We called it a learning contract. We got rid of the hierarchy and made our whole premise a co-learning process. This felt familiar to me, like the negotiations between the development and the church when I was becoming the Roving Listener.

This is the way relationships work. And communities may not often realize it, but we can talk about the practices of abundance.

As I mentioned before, we didn't hold meetings inside institutions (even the church), and we weren't going to hold the community's meetings at the foundation either. We needed to do all we could to balance the power.

The foundation needed us more than they realized. They understood relationships inside the walls of their building, but they did not understand, as we did, the effect of the foundation's work within the walls of community and neighborhood.

We would take learning journeys together, both inside and outside our city, and learn new ways of cultivating relationships. The first year was just courting each other. It took time, and it was a little messy, but it was real.

Joy was a big part of our conversations at the ambassador meetings. A lot of the conversations were about Black-on-Black violence. Since we had started flipping the script, Pam would begin our check-ins by asking, "What brings you joy?" Several ambassadors said that institutions would often paint the neighborhoods as joyless.

We talked about ways to carve out a portion of our work that centered joy. Pam went back to Brian and a couple of the foundation's leaders about the foundation's role in helping to center joy in our work.

She pulled together some entrepreneurs, ambassadors, and party throwers to create the Black Joy Festival (now going on seven years!).

The first year 2,000 people showed up. A crowd this size would usually only show up for communal grieving and anger at a site of violence. Not this time.

The only thing being celebrated was one another—community, resilience, and one another's gifts. It was so successful that the foundation put more money into it. In the second year, 5,000 people showed up. That year, the city council declared a day in late July "Black Joy Day." It has continued to grow, with over 10,000 people descending on Riverside Park.

Seana the Weaver

The ambassadors are still around, even after all the changes the years bring. Some thought it would blow away after a couple of years. The power of relationships created a natural organizing that took capital and turned it into currency. The change in leadership shifted the essence of the work from an institutional end, yet the essence of the relationships that were created has deepened its roots and multiplied its fruit.

Seana, my co-author here, joined me in the work with the ambassadors. I needed her expertise with institutions. Before this, I hadn't spent much time with Seana, except through church and our mutual friendship with Mike.

One of the first things she had the ambassadors do was create guiding principles. They included:

- **Act in abundance, not a scarcity mindset.** We are our own power. When we see a need in the community, we do everything in our power to look first in our own communities and networks for possible solutions. If we can't find the resources, answers, and connections there, we inquire about our social capital. When helping a person in need, we also ask them about their gifts.

- **Integrity in human relationships.** We seek to cultivate relationships. Above all, we listen—not just to what people say, but to what they do. We treat people with dignity. We enter these relationships believing in their capabilities and their stories.

- **Equity.** We advocate for equitable access to and distribution of resources, for money that flows to the people who need it, and for sharing social capital.

- **Engage human assets.** We identify and nourish people's gifts through their hands, head, heart, and what brings them joy. There is more to our stories than what we lack, and honoring the unique gifts we bring lets us thrive in the face of adversity.

- **Imagination.** While we all deal with complex issues, we think beyond the usual ways of solving problems. The answers have to go beyond the status quo. Taking risks is an important part of our work, so long as it's legal and safe.
- **Work alongside community.** Everything we do should be done alongside the community—nothing about us without us. That means we seek invitation into a community, actively listening and amplifying its voice. We advocate for and with our community, and we keep learning about others.
- **Ambassador, not employee.** This collective of organizers and community leaders maintains a partnership with the Indianapolis Foundation—a relationship with boundaries that honor the group's expertise and autonomy in running the collective itself. The partnering organization is not positioned to dictate to the collective, and the collective is not bound by institutional framework or hierarchy.

Seana is a weaver of the fabric of community. She joined me shortly after the ambassador work began. When I approached her to partner with me, I was surprised and thrilled that she was willing—though she came with her usual skepticism.

Seana was key for checking power and making sure it was authentically shared, not just tokenized. She posed the best questions for entering our contract. One of them was what the foundation was willing to give up and share with the ambassadors.

Seana asked, "Who are you willing to learn from?" This was about balancing the power. We got rid of the question about money. She made it clear: we don't lead with money. Relationships come first, along with a willingness to be honest about the disparities and inequities.

Seana's needle was precise and piercing. The ambassadors met twice a month, once in the community and once at the Indianapolis Foundation. Our meetings were set up to start with love. Seana would have us begin by loving on one another. She asked, "Who are we bringing along with us?" (Each ambassador always brought two neighbors along.)

Seana would have us ask, "What needs to be called out?" These meetings always happened around a meal. It was important for people at the Indianapolis Foundation to see us interact this way. It was a brilliant strategy: it took the power and made it visible to the rest of the Indianapolis Foundation.

The second meeting each month was to meet people in the community, from the mayor's office to those who are often invisible. We celebrated individual community members and their gifts. A lot of these meetings were very tense, especially when we met with "public servants" or "city officials."

Seana and I would often get calls from Pam and Brian saying the ambassadors were putting heat on institutions around town. (Two of the ambassadors were downstairs protesting while Brian and Pam met with the very people they were protesting.) City officials particularly targeted the ambassadors who were outside protesting.

This is important. This is how we proved we were balancing the power.

One of our earliest relationships was with Deputy Mayor Jeff Bennett. This was right at the beginning of the pandemic, when tons of money was being hoarded by social service organizations. People were out of work and couldn't pay rent—service workers in particular.

The deputy mayor wanted to talk with the ambassadors to find solutions for getting the money into the right people's hands. The conversation became tense immediately, because Jeff asked the ambassadors about getting the word out about the social service organizations.

The ambassadors immediately responded by pointing back to their guiding principles. The money needed to go more directly into people's hands, and they needed to be treated with dignity.

One of the biggest reasons the money wasn't leaving the hands of social service agencies is that they didn't have relationships with families in their neighborhoods (which the ambassadors did). The agencies had names in file cabinets. The ambassadors had them in their hearts.

The other thing the ambassadors pushed back on was the form people had to fill out to get the money. The form was excruciating, both in length and in asking unimportant questions. The nonprofits wouldn't even reach out to the very people they were supposed to be supporting.

After the third meeting, the ambassadors came with a proposal: redo the form with just the basic information needed, plus three questions: (1) What brings you joy? (2) What are you good enough to teach someone else how to do? (3) What two people do you have who support you? It usually took thirty days to get a check. We guaranteed we could get the money out in five days.

What Does It Mean for Institutions to Be Good Neighbors?

With the success we had moving those funds for the city, we built trust within the foundation's ecosystem. Pam, Seana, and I were able to push the community foundation to create a more robust grant-making process. It didn't overhaul its grant-making entirely, but it carved out money that could be community- and neighbor-driven.

This happened in two ways. On the foundation's side, a fund called the Neighborhood Relief Fund was created to nudge the nonprofits receiving funding to get to know their neighbors.

They had to get to know the neighbors and people they were serving. The ambassadors and the foundation would follow up with a neighbor to verify the nature of the relationship. The nonprofits that developed meaningful relationships and friendships got the grant.

In some of the calls, the ambassadors would find out whether the nonprofits actually knew any of the neighbors they were serving. We gave them names of residents, and sometimes the center never called the people at all.

The second process was one we took from the second round of city grants, which we called the Joy Fund. We borrowed it from our joy fund at Broadway Church. (The church had done away with its "emergency assistance fund" and replaced it with a "joy fund.") It had the same premise: people and neighbors were already doing something, already making contributions to their community. We wanted to know what they were doing to support the community—and they couldn't be doing it alone. It let the city and the foundation celebrate their citizens' gifts.

Our work was always about recognizing community and inviting it to grow. That's why we asked, "What two other people support you?" The ambassadors couldn't do something for someone else; instead, they put money into the hands of people in the neighborhood who already had power and agency.

Some of those projects—for example, with Valerie Davis—funded a local entrepreneur to put on a Black vegan festival. Kiana, the vegan, had done a few smaller, local events, but Valerie used her connections to turn it into a busy street festival. Two thousand people showed up on the first day.

This was powerful because people came who didn't usually come to a vegan fest. They didn't come just to eat vegan food but to visit all the vendors and celebrate the gifts of the community.

This shaped the nature of the community foundation's work. They began to see the community as their real partners. The vendors weren't nonprofits; they were the genuine article, the real neighbors, the real deal.

Sometimes it was a struggle with the money, because people didn't really believe you wanted to put it in the hands of the people in the community. Like they often say at churches, "We've never done it that way before."

The work seemed to be going really well. It was strong. The relationships were beginning to take root.

Change Is Constant

Something happened we did not see coming: Brian Payne retired. It was a big moment. We really learned how important authentic relationships are. Things started to change when new leadership walked in. They didn't have to fall apart, but the change of leadership at the community foundation changed the nature of the work. What stayed true is that we were public with our stories, and we held to our guiding principles.

We realized institutions could be good neighbors only if the people in leadership were committed to deep, meaningful relationships—and to the framework of joy.

Rob MacPherson, from the Central Indiana Community Foundation, says:

> We thought we had institutionalized this culture, but what we've learned is that you don't institutionalize culture. You cultivate relationships that build up associational life and meaningful friendships. That's what makes institutions good neighbors.

When presidents changed, power shifted. The relationship between the community, the ambassadors, and the Indianapolis Foundation began to shift.

The first new leader came from the corporate world. We started to shift back into the mindset that the institution had all the expertise and wanted to support the community by hoarding all the giving.

In hindsight, one of the lessons is that this work can't be done by any institution alone. It also can't be done by residents alone, or by government alone. It needs everyone in the ecosystem—not just to work together but to take learning journeys together.

The institutions couldn't see it because of scarcity—the fear that they wouldn't exist if they didn't do things the way they always had. There was fear that taking too much time would stop progress. Leadership changed across the board. (Pam Ross left for another venture, among others.)

Yet because of the work we have done—as with the Black Joy Festival—we know our children, our grandchildren, and their grandchildren will have an awareness of their giftedness and power woven deeply into the fabric of their communities. The epigenetics of joy are in our hands, our hearts, our actions.

CHAPTER 7

Starting from Scratch

Seana Murphy

In a former life, I ran early childhood education centers. Due to restrictions, we were not able to purchase modeling dough. Not to be deterred, we made our own. Following a recipe, we created the sticky malleable substance and allowed the children the freedom to play without fear. Using very basic ingredients, we were able to create, from scratch, a simple substance that provided hours of laughter and joy for adults and children.

"Dance to the Music" starts from scratch. The ingredients outlined in the beginning of the song are simple:

> All we need is a drummer . . .
> I'm gonna add a little guitar[1]

A drum, a guitar, and later in the song a bass, organ, horn, and a message combine to create a song to which I surrender with joy that the calling out of the ingredients and mixing of the sounds stir up in my bones.

I am not a cook. I find no joy in cooking. I do, however, find joy in watching my mother, sisters, and friends cook. Biscuits, cakes, and breads are all made from scratch with each ingredient carefully measured and added as called for most times. The beauty of watching my family cook is in seeing the liberties that each one takes with the recipe. A dash of this, a little bit more of that, maybe not so much of this . . . these words waft across the kitchen as they put together the masterpiece. The beauty is that the masterpiece though tied to the recipe is liberated by the imagination and curiosity of the cooks. It is also created with the expectation of the unexpected. The risk of altering a recipe is that the item will not turn out as prescribed. Therein lies the beauty of it all.

It is interesting to witness people move in joy and freedom. The two elements—joy and freedom—allow people to risk with ease. The what if's that prevent people from trying new things fall away. Changing a recipe is risky. Changing one ingredient will change the result. Yet creating from scratch eases trepidation and wonderful concoctions are created.

When we work from the framework of imagination, 100 year work opens up unexplored vistas that can yield unimagined results. The invitation to imagination is an invitation to the portals of joy and freedom. In this vortex, working in flow, a new reality can be created.

There is no singular recipe for 100 years work. There are, however, ingredients that are needed to begin and to sustain the work. The list below and accompanying stories is illustrative, not exhaustive.

Love

Though the expression and sentiment has been cheapened, love is a key ingredient. It is not the main ingredient, for in a recipe all ingredients play an important, singular role in bringing everything together.

In the early 1980s, my mother and a few members of the church were pulled together for a conversation. This was an effort to build relationships between residents in the community and church commuters. During the course of the conversation, two of the women involved found a commonality; both were nurses. Throughout the course of several conversations, my mom and Jan decided to share their skills and talents with the community.

Every Saturday morning, Jan would drive into the neighborhood, meet up with Ernestine (my mother), and provide no-cost health support to members in the community.

One Saturday, the meanest lady in the neighborhood came in for a screening. This woman had forbidden her grandchildren from playing with "that dyke" (me). She made a habit of calling the police on my stepfather, who was known to grow weed in between the sunflower and tomato plants as part of our family garden, and she delighted in taking the kickball from children whenever the ball landed in her yard.

She entered into the Bridge House without speaking, filled out the form, and demanded to have her blood pressure checked. My mother, the mother of the dyke, took her blood pressure and gasped. My mother looked the woman in her eyes and asked her how she was feeling?

"Why?" was her response.

My mother calmly stated, "Your blood pressure is in the stroke range. How are you feeling?"

"I am fine," the woman protested.

"You need to get this checked," my mother persisted. After a thirty-second silent standoff, the woman relented with: "How am I supposed to see a doctor? I ain't got no car."

My mother retorted, "I will take you whenever and wherever you need to go." Jan stepped in and said, "You need to go today."

My mother took a deep breath and said, "Come on."

Our family was poor. We were so poor that the thought of an unanticipated ride raised real concerns about having enough gas or gas money to make it through to the next paycheck.

Nevertheless, my mother took this mean woman, her neighbor, to the emergency room and sat with her until she was seen, medication was provided, and she was sent home. I imagine that sitting in the emergency room for hours felt like 100 years for both of them. I imagine that there were awkward silences, inappropriate statements made about others in the emergency room, and secret prayers sent to God begging simultaneously for the woman's blood pressure issue to be addressed and for the doctors to hurry up and do it!

This is how love for the community; love for one's neighbor shows up. It is not romantic. This love makes no guarantees of happy beginnings or happy endings. This is a lived love. It is a love that understands that close relationship is not required in order to act from a place of empathy. It is a knowing love. It is a love that knows that even the meanest person deserves to be seen, heard, and cared for. It is a resilient love. It is a love that recognizes that this work is hard and that love is the primary ingredient. PS: The woman, after getting the medical care, continued to call me a dyke. She continued to call the police on my stepfather and take kickballs from children. She did not return to the Bridge House with a plate of cookies and a warm thank you nor did she give my mother gas money. She didn't stop being who she was.

The simple lesson in this story is that love is centered, not the desired hero effect that drives many to do this work.

I first experienced this type of love as a middle and high school student. At the time, Broadway United Methodist Church ran an expansive recreation program. Bob Goler and Thaddeus Starks were the leaders. Between the two men, countless number of basketball, kickball, and softball games were played. Between the two men, girls and boys were exhausted every day from activities. Between the two men, the idea of going to college was seeded in my brain. I was a poor Black girl in whom they saw leadership potential.

I could not appreciate what they saw at the time as evidenced by the number of times I literally cursed them for missing a call in any game. I could not appreciate their love for me because I did not recognize the young woman whom they saw. My cursing, fighting, and violent emotional outbursts did not deter them from pressing me about the future. Future? I lived on 29th and Park in the middle of the crack epidemic. What future did they see? What were they not seeing?

Many events transpired over the course of their time in the community. I know, however, that it was their *love* that kept them pushing harder whenever I pushed back. It was not romantic. I disappointed both men when I decided against their wishes not to attend a historically Black college.

The disappointment, however, did not prevent them from checking in, through the grapevine, to ensure that I was "minding myself" and "doing what I needed to do." I never thanked them for harassing me about hanging out too late or for too long with friends from the neighborhood. I never thanked them for pulling me away from the many fistfights that I welcomed. I never thanked them at all. This did not prevent them from loving. Love in the grittiest sense of the word is an ingredient, a necessary and powerful ingredient, yet not the only ingredient that is needed.

Power

Dr. Rufus Burrows Jr. was my mentor in this dimension and is now my spirit guide (along with others) on the ancestral plane. I love him. Rufus was a personalist in every sense of the word. He believed in the personality of God and in the personhood of everyone.

Rufus and I argued incessantly about reason and will. My question to Rufus at the time was, Is it reasonable to expect reason in an unreasonable situation? Is it free will if the only choices available are unreasonable? These questions are esoteric in nature but led me to examine and to develop an ontology of power that asserts that everyone has power. Awareness of this fact is a key ingredient in the work.

Oftentimes when power is discussed it is framed in the context of money. Money is a form of power. Access, however, is as powerful as money. The two combined are at the crux of inequities.

People who do not have money have power: the power of influence, the power of choice, and the power of action. Institutions self-sustain by creating codependence that is predicated on convincing people of their lack of power. Throughout my work in community, however, I have witnessed what can happen when the power of the alleged poor is harnessed.

For a decade, I ran Indiana's 21st Century Scholars program. This program was designed to financially support students meeting certain criteria with accessing postsecondary education. Adopted by the state of Indiana in 1991, the 21st Century Scholars program required parent engagement in that students could not sign up for or complete the program without the parent's signature. The early stages of program implementation mirrored the work that continues across communities: parent meetings.

The parent meetings consisted of an "expert" talking *to* (not with) parents about the importance of students keeping the 21st Century Scholars pledge and the financial benefits that come with completing college. This one-dimensional approach to parent engagement resulted in more conversations about the meeting food menu than about anything of real significance.

When I hired in as the state director, my first ill-conceived idea was to abolish food. The consequence of this action was immediate. Staff members and parents contacted the federal program officer to register their complaints. The officer in turn called me, questioned the decision, and directed me to offer a compromise. It was in that moment that I realized the parents were key to the success of the program. The parents were organized, knowledgeable, and unafraid.

After a second incident with parents, I knew that we needed to build an infrastructure that celebrated this power. The second incident happened on a Saturday afternoon when I received a call from a supervisor questioning why parents were standing outside of a grocery store selling baked goods. I had no idea.

I drove over to the grocery store and saw card tables filled with homemade goods and little price stickers. When I approached the parent who was leading the sale and asked what was going on, her response was simple: The program doesn't pay for books and these babies will need them when they go to college.

I had no counterargument with this fact. I did, however, advise her that the grocery store requires an agreement with vendors. She rolled her eyes and told me that she didn't know this and they would leave once the goods were sold or if they are made to leave by the store manager.

The parents didn't ask for permission from the program nor did they ask for permission from the grocery store. They decided and they acted. They had power and they used it. Their action paved the way for the establishing of Dollars for Scholars chapters across the state. This parent-led organization raised money and awarded book scholarships for students.

The experiences with the parents taught me very valuable lessons. The first lesson: blindness is real. In my effort to assert my understanding of "what should happen in meetings," I used power over the parents and paid an immediate consequence. The second lesson, listening to and with those whom one is to "serve," frees the imagination and lowers the fear of risk-taking. As a result of the lessons, I worked with an incredible team of parents and my good friend Allison to develop a structure that hired sixteen parents as full-time employees of the program and ninety-two stipend-paid parent volunteers. The only jobs required of the parents were to talk with other parents about the program and to assist any parent with completing the paperwork needed to secure and use the scholarship.

The idea of hiring parents, with the only requirement being that the parent had a child in the program, did not go over well with other program staff members nor with the host institutions across the state. It was a very difficult endeavor.

The difficulty was rooted in the meritocracy that correlates educational achievement with ability, employability, and worth. Convinced of the importance of the strategy and using data (parent meeting evaluations that did not reference food, increased numbers of parents attending college visits, and the number of students completing the program and enrolling into college), I, along with the team, refused to relent. The refusal to relent resulted in the 21st Century Scholars Parent Leaders training other program officials across the country on how to effectively engage parents!

The success of this program component cannot be understated. The parents lived, worked, and loved in the same communities as the parents that program had to reach. Conversations and workshops took place in homes; at local restaurants and churches; and basketball and football games. By deinstitutionalizing the program, thousands of students graduated from high school and entered into college.

During the course of my time with the program, I would remind students, state officials, and secondary school and college-level administrators of the fact that parents had the power. Parents had to sign their students up for the program. Parents had to complete the application for financial aid. Parents had to accompany students on college visits, and so on. It was in everyone's best interest to talk with and to parents because parents had the power.

Since my time with the program, many changes have taken place. These changes were driven by the unanticipated success of the program. Program officials did not expect success. Program officials did not anticipate colleges and universities coming alongside the program to provide the funding and support needed to ensure student success once on the college campus.

Program officials did not expect that a small group of parents could commandeer the support of community foundations, Lions Clubs, and other philanthropic organizations to provide money, internship, and other opportunities to "low-income" students across the state.

The program requirements changed to erect barriers that prevent students from receiving 100 percent of the award. Of the changes, means testing—proving that one is as poor at that point in time as the day that they signed up for the program—is particularly troubling. What has not changed is the proof represented in the success of the program: It was connection, not the promise of tuition, that mattered to families. Another thing that has not changed is that there are parents in every part of the state who know how to talk about and how to navigate the college-going systems. The parents know this because many moons ago, they were hired to do two jobs: talk about the program and assist any parent with navigating the system.

Many years ago, I sat in on a clearness circle with a young man who was struggling with a situation on his job. A clearness circle is the Quaker practice of allowing the person seeking clarity to sit among a trusted group of friends who can only ask the individual questions. Participants do not offer advice. As the time progressed and questions were asked, it occurred to me that the individual had been convinced of the fact that they lacked power.

As the time wound down, I asked my final question: Where is your power in this? Rooted in the question was the assumption that the individual had power. Power is an important ingredient. Power presents in many different ways across different groups. Power is never neutral. The decision to use or not to use/to act or not act is always operative.

Imagination

Reinhold Niebuhr coined the phrase "the impossible possibility." I love the paradox represented in the phrase because it literally defines imagination. The impossible possibility of a system of human beings working in concert to live out the promise of "heaven on earth" unleashes a multicolored rush of joy in my brain.

As a black woman in this country, I know that the impossible possibility can be realized. The election of Barack Obama in 2008 is evidence of the impossible possibility realized. During my first year of college [1987], I was asked what I was planning to do upon graduation and I responded, "I plan to become the president of the United States." My classmates snickered and my professor rolled his eyes. In their minds that was impossible.

Travel back in time when slaves worked, sang, and prayed for freedom. The idea of a Black president was an impossible possibility yet today, we speak of the former president as though it was a normal occurrence in the life of a country rooted in genocide and slavocracy.

Imagination takes courage. It is not enough to dream of what could be. The dream must be acted upon. During the pandemic, I worked with a group of residents to determine what they wanted to see in the community. Over and above anything else, they wanted to have a seat and voice at tables where decisions about the community were being made. Several residents stated that they dreamed about speaking directly to officials and directing where money flowed in the community.

Across the course of several weeks and conversations, the resident grant-making committee was established. This group of residents invited other residents to apply for $3,000 grants that could be used to showcase their talents with others in the community. One of the conditions of the grant was that the applicants paid themselves for the work. The committee met and reviewed grants on a monthly basis. One hundred percent of the applicants were awarded grants. The committee celebrated each applicant and themselves. They were able to make decisions about where money flowed and this changed their understanding of power and voice.

On November 18, 2010, two Black sister friends established the GirlTrek movement. The mission/vision of the movement is to increase the lifespan of Black and Brown women across the country. Today, the movement is 1,371,776 members, representing 7 percent of the total population of African American women.

GirlTrek invited and invites Black women to heal our bodies, inspire our daughters, and reclaim our communities through the simple act of walking! Two women, neither of whom are trained medical professionals, combined courage and imagination to develop a plan of action to address the health issues affecting Black women across the country. "Never ask for permission to save your own life!" is the motto. The beauty and gift of this organization is that it is unapologetically designed with, for, and about Black women. The invitation to participate is simple: lace up your sneakers, walk fifteen minutes in one direction, and fifteen minutes back for a total of thirty minutes per day. Brilliant.

The impact of the movement must be situated in the traditional advice from doctors across the spectrum when addressing the critical health issues that are ravaging the Black female community: obesity, high blood pressure, and diabetes. Traditional advice, in addition to prescription drugs, remains eat less, exercise more.

This advice ignores the historical trauma that Black women carry in our bodies. It ignores the importance of community—connection—and love that is needed to motivate and to maintain change. Morgan and Vanessa (GirlTrek founders) understood and understand the importance of addressing the body as the temple.

They continually acknowledge that while we carry trauma in our bodies, we do not and will not amplify this above *joy*! Imagine hearing this from a doctor. Can you imagine a doctor prescribing a nine-day Prayer Trek as a healing modality?

Can you imagine engaging with a medical professional who has the ability to call out *joy* in the midst of a medical crisis? GirlTrek's work is transformative because it is rooted in community. It is transformative because the movement combined imagination with power and created an atmospheric change in communities all around the country and the world.

The impossible possibilities are materialized when people, in this case two beautiful Black women, have the courage to dream (and live into being our ancestors' wildest dream), acknowledge their own power, and call forward the power that is alive in the spirits of others.

The outcomes of this movement are proof (not that it is required) that collective healing rooted in love and power is possible.

GirlTrek has become one of the most effective public health interventions in the country. In our most recent member survey (2019):

- 61 percent of Black women lost weight;
- 90 percent experienced fewer symptoms of depression;
- 28 percent were prescribed less medication that year than previous years;
- 59percent walk daily at life-saving levels (according to the CDC, five days per week for thirty minutes); and
- 56 percent have sustained a habit of daily walking for more than one year.

Additional information about this important social justice movement can be found at www.girltrek.org.

Willingness to Fail

I don't know anyone who embraces failure as part of the journey. In April 2012, Google announced the Google Glass product. The glasses provided an augmented reality experience through lenses that immediately accessed data from the internet, cell phones, and other digital data sources. The company spent $400 million on the glasses and abandoned the project two years later. This by any definition is a significant failure. Innovation requires failure. The inequity in the failure runway for many institutions stifles innovation thus reinforcing failures just on a lower scale. Initial phases of the 21st Century Scholars program were failures. The number of students enrolling in the program was low. The number of students going to college was low. The number of students staying beyond the first semester in college was low. Over the course of years—after trying many iterations of the program infrastructure—the program began to improve. It was not, however, until the parents were hired and positioned to connect with other parents did the program explode.

I deliberately omitted an explicit statement of the 21st Century Scholars program requirements. In 1991, students qualifying for free/reduced-price lunch enrolled in the program by signing the 21st Century Scholars pledge:

- I will remain crime, drug, and alcohol free.
- I will graduate from high school with a cumulative GPA of 2.0 on a 4.0 scale.
- I will apply on time for federal and state financial aid,
- I will apply for acceptance into an accredited Indiana college, university, or proprietary school.

This program was habitually compared to another program that focused on middle-income families that boasted a 90 percent high school graduation rate and an 85 percent college-going rate among the students served. Whenever the comparison was made in my presence, I would counter and state that a program with all of the advantages afforded families from the middle/upper middle classes should have better outcomes. Anything less than 100 percent is a failure.

Failure can be a gift as it can free one from the burden of expectations. Failure should be encouraged. In most instances where people are doing the work of joy and abundance, systems have already failed so the worst outcome is that you join an impressive lot. Failure should be welcomed as an opportunity to try new things and an opportunity to further examine the ways in which power is used to set people up for success. What matrix is being used? Who developed the matrix? Are the right things being measured? These are all questions that a good, old-fashioned failure pushes to the top.

CHAPTER 8

Rising from the Ashes

Seana Murphy

The first day of the first year of school, for parents, is fraught with anxiety. All the what if's; the "Did I remember to?" and "Will my child know to?" fill the mind blinding parents to the anxious excitement of the child. The first day of the first year of school is a dichotomy in time. It is the only time that children go without bias into an unfamiliar space wide open to all possibilities. It is also the day that institutions begin the process of closing children off to all possibilities. This is a brutal yet real truth. On this day, the first day, children embody the ingredients for institutional change referenced throughout this book. Children are curious about other children and their environment. They are hungry for knowledge. They are mesmerized by the changing of colors, the metamorphosis of caterpillars into butterflies. Every relationship is essential to their existence in the world. Abundance and possibility are alive in their spirits.

Throughout the course of this book, an invitation to see and behave differently is extended. The stories of possibility are situated in the 100-year timeline. The stories of actuality are positioned in the now thus contradicting the 100-year timeline. The contradiction encapsulates the truth of the work. The stories illuminate undiagnosed blindness and offer potential antidotes. The book does not deal with the contemporary question of reformation versus revolution.

The book deals with the social, emotional, and spiritual question of resurrection. If we as authors have made one point across the different voices, perspectives, and lived experiences, it is that the idea of adjectives ending with the word *less* used to describe another human is an illusion. There are no "less than" humans. There are, however, unseen, unheard, unwelcomed, and so forth, but no "less than" human. This is an important distinction because the "less than" (powerless, voiceless) adjectives are gentle yet brutal ways of blaming the oppressed for the exercise of power over that happens. Whereas the description of "un" means that power brokers are choosing not to see, hear, or respond. This delicate shift in the narrative places the responsibility for examining and changing institutional practices and structures square in the lap of those who construct, build, and sustain oppressive institutions and practices.

There are 161 years of pain, love, joy, and celebration represented in the lives of the authors. At some point the years melded together and we became friends. Our histories are intricately connected from our ancestral roots to our complicated relationship of today. When we met, there were no intake forms. When we met, there was no needs assessment. When we met, there were no voyeuristic questions about past experiences. When we met there simply was "the first day of the first year of school energy."

Our meeting was **intentional**. Mike called for me to come into his office. I **deliberately** sought out DeAmon over the course of time, **we decided to cultivate the relationship that eventuated into friendship.** Each one of us has a distinct relationship with one another. We fight with and for one another. Everyday we choose to hold one another in love—with compassion—while pushing one another to live into the fullness of this life. Sometimes, it is romantic. Other times it is hard, yet we decide to remain intentional and deliberate in the cultivation of the friendship.

We return to day two of the first year of school. We go to the playground of life and seek one another out because we know and understand that loving connection is the comfort in the storms of anxiety, insecurity, and disappointment that working in this way in this world can bring.

Black church music is a teaching tool in this work. The song "For the Good of Them" (best version is Rev. Milton Brunson and The Thompson Community Singers) captures the unadulterated truth of this book. It begins with the oft-quoted scripture "The race is not given to the swift or to the strong. Further into the song, the facts of 100 years' work are laid out-sometimes, you may have to cry and sometimes you may have to walk alone. Of the difficulties that one experiences in this work, the sometimes moments are the hardest.

Crying, walking alone, barely believing in the impossible possibilities is hard. In these moments reason fails and the waves of catastrophic questions emerge: What are we doing? What difference are we really making? Why do our efforts fall on blind eyes and deaf ears? This is all part of the work. I have a quote from Gabrielle Roth stuck to the wall of my bathroom by the mirror. The positioning of the quote is such that I cannot look into the mirror without seeing it. It says:

> In many shamanic societies, if you came to a medicine person complaining of being disheartened, dispirited, or depressed, they would ask one of four questions: "When did you stop dancing? When did you stop singing? When did you stop being enchanted by stories? When did you stop being comforted by the sweet territory of silence?"

The questions bring me back to centering on abundance and joy. These questions can and should be asked of people in everyday conversations. The power of the questions is the reminder of how beautiful life, in all of the complications, is. The questions simultaneously point to the past, acknowledge the present, and point to the future in which joy is alive.

In 2018, Broadway United Methodist Church, with the support from the Center for Congregations, hosted city-wide discussions on racism. The series "Interrupting Racism" consisted of book studies, learning journeys, and screenings of the Netflix specials *The New Jim Crow* and *When They See Us*. The small group responsible for leveraging the funds and implementing the process spent countless hours together, planning and coordinating the year-long experience. Throughout the course of the series, members of the congregation and members of the community gathered together for meals and conversation. The stories of racial terror were heart-wrenching. The resistance to this level of truth telling was heavy. The participants of all races were weary yet each session ended with each person making a commitment to justice. The actual experiences, in the moment, were not joyful. However, the intentionality of starting with meals and sharing about the day-to-day highs and lows in life created an atmosphere for the development of strong human connection.

Prior to the screening of *When They See Us*, the group hired four Black social workers, a jazz singer, and other musicians. The social workers were hired to support anyone feeling overwhelmed due to the psychological and physical violence captured in the series. The musicians were asked to bring instruments that participants would use to release the emotional energy that arises when watching the film. The singer led voice experiments that culminated in the creation of a communal sound.

During the first screening of *When They See Us*, a young woman wept quietly before leaving the room. A Black female social worker followed and offered to talk with her. During the conversation the young woman revealed that a person in attendance had violently sexually assaulted her in high school. The social worker said very little to the woman. She simply held on to her as she cried.

After consoling her, the social worker walked the woman to her car and offered her personal phone number along with the invitation to call whenever, if ever, she needed.

During this same episode, my twelve-year-old son literally folded into my arms and cried as he witnessed the injustice unfolding on the screen. I said nothing. I held him in my arms.

At the conclusion of the episode, people grabbed small drums, rain sticks, tambourines, drumsticks, and other instruments and walked around the room shaking, beating, drumming, and moving the energy out of their bodies. Shortly after, the jazz singer invited each person to make a sound with their voice. She strung each sound together until a song was born. She then invited participants to clap and hold the sound that they had made. At the end of the evening, because of and in spite of racial terrorism, a joyful noise was made.

> Have you ever gone astray . . .
> Have you ever lost your way
> —Edie Brickell, "Go Where the Love Is"[1]

I was introduced to this song through my son Matthew who, at the ripe old age of ten, recognized the significance of the words and eagerly shared it with me after having learned it from his teacher. We were growing through a difficult time. Sherrell—his birth mom, and an incredible mother—was exhausted having spent all of her emotional strength fighting the childhood cancer that had crept into Matthew's body at the age of two and lingered until his eighth birthday. She waged the battle while working full-time and going to school full-time. I was coming out of a heartbreaking love that abruptly ended, concluding the work with the 21st Century Scholars program, and preparing to make a career change. Mike and DeAmon held all of us in prayer. DeAmon offered opportunities for Matthew to hang out with other young men who were living with loving women yet missing the fathers that they had never known.

At that time, Matthew did not have a full understanding of all that had happened in his body. He was behaving as a typical young, Black male child.

He was smarting off, disrupting boring classes at school, and giving both of us the blues at every turn as he had become accustomed to getting what he wanted when he wanted it. I was stressed. I was worried about the relationship between Matthew and Sherrell. Co-parenting is difficult. It is even more difficult if the relationships between the parents and the child are strained.

At the advice of a friend and therapist, I booked a trip for the three of us to Washington, DC. This was an idea to allow space for the creation of new foundations in our relationships. It was while Matthew and Sherrell were walking ahead of me that I heard him singing this song as he held her hand. In that moment, in the spaces where their palms met, Matthew knew where the love was and is. The trip did not result in a magical turnaround and we are still working on strengthening our relationships. The trip was, however, a reminder that we have to go where the love is.

Shawna Wells, CEO of Wells Coaching, is the personification of Maya Angelou's phenomenal woman. Shawna is my coach. Shawna is thirteen-plus years my junior yet she is my teacher. I have learned more about love and centering love in practical ways from Shawna over the last few months than I have from the unreasonable number of romantic relationships that I have engaged in over the years. During a conversation with Shawna, she shared that the reason why she got into the business of coaching came about because when she asked Black women what they are good at, the question was met with silence. The silence was then followed by the typical responses that most share: the ideas and beliefs of others.

Shawna's expectation when asking the question is deeper than the litany that we are capable of producing. Her expectation is that we pause and reflect on the universal, ancestral, and divine and then name what we are good at. The degree of insight, the ability to witness to the inherent abundance that exists in Black women, is love. It is transformative. It is necessary.

Throughout the course of this book, we have attempted to demonstrate how and where abundance lives, breathes, and has its being in communities that are often unseen and unheard. Throughout this book, love has been centered; love in all of its manifestations and complexities. Romantic, messy, agape, selfish, faithful, divine, and all of the other adjectives ascribed love are reflected in the book.

The reason for the centering of love is simple. When embarking on the journey to witness, act, and enact abundance, the questions and answers about love are critical. What/who do you love enough to act with, to effect the change that you want to see in this world? Where is the love right now? Can you see it? If it is hiding, who can guide you to it? Who loves you enough to hold you in times of celebration and tribulation? The answers to these questions will guide your journey.

CHAPTER 9

Learning from the Illuminators

Michael Mather

As I have written here, at First United Methodist Church of Boulder we hired two people who live on the street to identify the gifts, talents, dreams, and passions of others who live on the street. We call them Illuminators.

In October of 2025, the Illuminators were reflecting on their year of work. It was fun to think about all the people we had met through them. We had met people living on the street who were former world-class BMX racers, classical trombone players, art teachers, a physician (!), chefs, and mental health workers—all of them also sisters and brothers, daughters and sons, mothers and fathers, even grandparents.

We also hired an "animador" to connect the gifts the Illuminators identified with social capital. Slowly but surely, this work has gone on, connecting people who live on the street—and people who don't—with photographers, cooks, people who love technology, artists, and more.

Travis, Nesti, Chris, and Gabe, all of whom served as Illuminators over the past year, were reflecting on the previous year.

In September of 2025, they had received a visit from the mayor, along with people from the police department, social services, the religious community, and another government office—all from a medium-sized midwestern city that wanted to learn from them.

When they were asked to speak to a communications class at the University of Colorado, one of the students asked, "What do you need from us?" Nesti answered, "We don't need anything from you. Except to be seen."

They had identified a lot of gifts in the lives of people on the street over the previous year. No surprise there. It was wonderful. The challenge is: how do we keep up with all the goodness, all the gifts around us? How do we move past housed people's prejudices, past our failure to see the rich history and stories of the people in front of us?

Then a revelation came. As they talked about the different people they had met and identified over the year, they began to count how many were now living indoors—not in shelters. They calculated that 80 percent of the people whose gifts they had identified were now housed.

The astonishing thing was that they had not worked on housing. That wasn't the role. They identify the gifts, talents, dreams, and passions of people. And as they have done that, people have gotten more connected and ended up finding places to live—finding themselves, altogether, on more solid ground.

More friends, more love, more laughter, more joy. Maybe there is something to this epigenetics of joy after all, and the Illuminators are recognizing it and building on it.

CHAPTER 10
A Testimony

De'Amon Harges

The stories you have just read—of Seana, Mike, and me—are testimonies, and in them miracles are constantly happening. They are stories of the fabric of the beloved community.

My best friend, the pastor of First United Methodist Church of Boulder, Colorado, created a testimony time as part of worship. He called it The Lesson from the Contemporary Church. (In announcing it, he would always add, "Because God didn't stop speaking when the book went to press, but continues to live in our lives and stories.") Testifying helps us remember our baptism. My testimony is part of centuries of testimonies from my ancestors, so testifying is in our DNA, our epigenetics.

My grandmother often shared her testimony with my cousins, my siblings, and me. She did it to be a light, guiding us out of the clutches of scarcity and into the fabric of joy, abundance, and loving friendships.

Growing up in neighborhoods on the west side of South Bend, Indiana, and in Chicago, Illinois—among neighbors who looked like me and had testimonies like mine—changed my life. Those testimonies are the gospel coming to life.

As a child, I found myself going to church with my friend and sometime accomplice. It was Easter Sunday, and after a very long sermon, the altar call finally came. I decided to answer it and get baptized.

At the altar, I sort of confessed my sins and proclaimed Jesus Christ as my Lord and Savior. After the formal ceremony, I was drowned in the waters of forgiveness. I thought to myself, "I guess now I'm saved," but I didn't feel any different. When I got to my grandparents' house, I rushed to tell my grandmother, with excitement, that I had been baptized. She paused, with a stern look on her face, and said, "You just went down a dry devil and came up a wet devil!"

She followed with, "It's not the water you were submerged in, it's the water inside you—the water of the Spirit. Remember where God is working through your neighbor."

Now that is the essence of the beauty of being a child of God.

Her wisdom and her stories in this book are testimonies that are part of my DNA. Over centuries, these stories lived through my ancestors: Julia Braylock, Isham Dupree, Aleck Braylock, Sharon Braylock, Mary Lee Love, Peter Love, and, last but not least, my grandmother Marie Braylock.

Today, stories of abundance live through people like my daughter DeJanea Harges, a witness to justice and humanity. Joy shows up in Jada and Jalen, who remind people they have gifts. Imagination shows up in my son McKeith, a scientist who imagines healing through art and science together. These stories also show up in the love and friendship of my good friends: Janine Robinson Harges, Mike Mather, Seana Murphy, Wildstyle, and Januarie, who all remind me that I am beloved.

I can hear my grandmother's voice saying: don't go down dry and come up wet—go down wet and stay wet. Listen for where God is always abundant through the lives of others. And remember, that didn't stop when the book went to press.

Notes

A Note from the Authors

1. Margaret Walker, "For My People," *This Is My Century: New and Collected Poems* (University of Georgia Press, 1989).

Introduction

1. Langston Hughes, "I Dream a World," in *The Collected Poems of Langston Hughes*, ed. Arnold Rampersad and David Roessel (Alfred A. Knopf, 1994), lines 5–6.

Chapter 2

1. Mary Oliver, "Sometimes," *Red Bird* (Beacon Press, 2008), 37.

Chapter 3

1. Martin Luther King, Jr., "How Long, Not Long," March 25, 1965, Alabama State Capitol.

2. Audre Lorde, "The Master's Tools Will Never Dismantle the Master's House," in *Sister Outsider: Essays and Speeches* (Crossing Press, 2007), 110–14.

Chapter 7

1. Sly & the Family Stone, "Dance to the Music," track 1 on *Dance to the Music*, Epic Records, 1968.

Chapter 8

1. Edie Brickell, "Go Where the Love Is," track on The Way Way Back (Music from the Motion Picture), Hollywood Records, 2013.

www.ingramcontent.com/pod-product-compliance
Lightning Source LLC
LaVergne TN
LVHW030819231026
850699LV00037B/486

* 9 7 8 1 7 9 1 0 4 1 4 6 5 *